BOURBON CURIOUS

BOURBON
Curious

A SIMPLE TASTING GUIDE FOR THE SAVVY DRINKER

FRED MINNICK

Steve —
May your bourbon
always be neat!

ZENITH
PRESS

To Oscar Leo, I look forward to enjoying your first bourbon
with you. When you turn twenty-one, of course.

Note to readers: Please enjoy bourbon responsibly.

First published in 2015 by Zenith Press, an imprint of Quarto Publishing Group USA Inc.,
400 First Avenue North, Suite 400, Minneapolis, MN 55401 USA

© 2015 Quarto Publishing Group USA Inc.
Text © 2015 Fred Minnick

All photographs by Fred Minnick except where noted otherwise.

The information in this book is true and complete to the best of our knowledge. All recom-
mendations are made without any guarantee on the part of the author or Publisher, who also
disclaims any liability incurred in connection with the use of this data or specific details.

We recognize, further, that some words, brand names, and designations mentioned herein
are the property of the trademark holder. We use them for identification purposes only.
This is not an official publication.

Zenith Press titles are also available at discounts in bulk quantity for industrial or
sales-promotional use. For details write to Special Sales Manager at Quarto Publishing
Group USA Inc., 400 First Avenue North, Suite 400, Minneapolis, MN 55401 USA.

To find out more about our books, visit us online at www.zenithpress.com.

ISBN: 978-0-7603-4740-9

Library of Congress Cataloging-in-Publication Data

Minnick, Fred, 1978-
  Bourbon curious : a simple tasting guide for the savvy drinker / Fred Minnick.
     pages cm
  Includes bibliographical references and index.
  ISBN 978-0-7603-4740-9 (plc)
  1. Bourbon whiskey. I. Title.
  TP605.M566 2015
  663'.52--dc23
                    2015005244

Acquisitions Editor: Elizabeth Demers
Project Manager: Madeleine Vasaly
Art Director: James Kegley
Cover Designer: Richard Korab
Layout: Erin Seaward-Hiatt

Printed in China

10 9 8 7 6 5 4 3 2

CONTENTS

PART ONE

HISTORY, LEGENDS, AND CONTEMPORARY TRUTHS

Please treat yourself. Pick up a bottle of bourbon, twist the cork off, and smell those sweet and succulent vanilla and caramel aromas. Delight in the cinnamon and nutmeg notes. Pour the russet-colored elixir into your glass—add ice if you like—and let this glorious bourbon journey begin.

Bourbon transcends ingredients and brand names. It embodies a culture, a feeling, and a sense of unity that draws friends together and brings foes to peace.

But with greatness comes misunderstanding. Despite being a core piece of Americana and instrumental in the US tax economy, bourbon is the most misunderstood product on liquor store shelves. Fantastic legends have misinformed consumers for more than a century about who, exactly, invented bourbon; distillery tours often misinform visitors with incorrect regulations and terms.

Then couple these troubling details with the macho know-it-all bar boor. "You like bourbon? Let me tell you about bourbon! It has to be made in Kentucky." This guy takes a dominant posture, because he's in the professor role, and he spews—and in some cases, spits—blatantly wrong information in your ear when all you want to do is drink the damn bourbon in peace. He "educates" bartenders, random people on the subway, and his mother's friends with atrocious "facts" he's unearthed on Wikipedia.

Bourbon professionals spend a lot of time cleaning up this arrogant guy's messes, and what amazes me is how sure some of these people are that they're right. At a neighborhood cocktail party, I approached somebody parroting the blatantly wrong fact that bourbon "must be two years old." As he slammed his red Solo cup down and tried to get tough, I realized two things: one, he had stinky breath, and two, he wasn't a guy who liked being told he was wrong.

The truth is that bourbon can be made anywhere in the United States, not just Kentucky, and in fact comes from New York, Wyoming, Indiana, and many other states. For a five-decade stretch in the twentieth century, Mexican distilleries also produced bourbon, which is one of the reasons US distillers pursued geographical protection in Congress. Bourbon itself has no age requirement, but to be labeled straight bourbon it must be at least two years old.

Because of bourbon's continued growth in popularity, the misinformed malcontents are spreading like a bad virus. Hopefully, this book will reach you before they do.

I hope *Bourbon Curious* will become your guide to this wonderful liquor, as well as to a tasting journey that pairs brands to the four most common flavor notes found in bourbon—caramel, cinnamon, grain, and nutmeg. It's my goal to give you information about bourbon you won't find on the Internet or on a label. Even if you're a longtime bourbon aficionado, I hope you'll find yourself saying, "I didn't know that."

Let's begin at the beginning. What is bourbon?

All bourbon is whiskey, but not all whiskey is bourbon. If this doesn't make sense to you, don't worry—you're not alone. The most common question in my Bourbon 101 classes is "What's the difference between bourbon and whiskey?" I've found the best way to answer this question without watching my audience fall asleep is to give a simple analogy. In the same way the word *car* covers a broad range of motor vehicles, from a slick cherry-red 1965 Ford Mustang to a dilapidated blue 1982 Nissan station wagon, *whiskey* is a broad term that can be further broken down into categories dictated by country of origin, grain, and aging process. In short, whiskey is just distilled beer that has been aged in barrels.

Scotch and bourbon are both whiskeys, but the similarities stop there. Scotch must be made in Scotland, and its celebrated grain is barley; bourbon must be made in the United States, and its primary grain is corn. Scotch whiskey's regulated categories are single malt, single grain, blended malt, blended scotch whiskey, and blended grain whiskey; bourbon's regulated categories are straight, blended, blended straight, and bottled-in-bond.

The US Alcohol and Tobacco Tax and Trade Bureau (TTB) defines some bourbon terms (see sidebar), while distillers frequently add production descriptions, such as "sour mash," "small batch," and "single barrel."

BOURBON TYPES

The US Alcohol and Tobacco Tax and Trade Bureau (TTB) is the Treasury Department's office that enforces alcohol regulations. Bourbon makes up a small percentage of their toil, but TTB agents ensure, or at least try to ensure, the proper labeling of bourbon. You can look up past label approvals at TTBonline.gov. With the exception of bottled-in-bond, the following definitions are summaries from the TTB guidebook but are not the full regulations.

BOURBON WHISKEY

"Whisk[e]y produced in the U.S. at not exceeding 80% alcohol by volume (160 proof) from a fermented mash of not less than 51 percent corn and stored at not more than 62.5% alcohol by volume (125 proof) in charred new oak containers"

Brand example: American Pride Bourbon Whiskey

STRAIGHT BOURBON WHISKEY

"Bourbon whisk[e]y stored in charred new oak containers for 2 years or more 'Straight Bourbon Whisk[e]y' may include mixtures of two or more straight bourbon whiskies provided all of the whiskies are produced in the same state"

Brand example: Maker's Mark Kentucky Straight Bourbon Whisky

BLENDED BOURBON WHISKEY

"Blended whiskey produced in the U.S. containing not less than 51% on a proof gallon basis (excluding alcohol derived from added harmless coloring, flavoring, or blending materials) straight bourbon whiskey"

Brand example: Old Hickory Great American Whiskey Blended Bourbon Whiskey

BLENDED STRAIGHT BOURBON WHISKEY

"A blend of straight whiskies produced in the U.S. consisting entirely of straight bourbon whiskies"

Brand example: High West Whiskey American Prairie Reserve Blend of Straight Bourbons

BOTTLED-IN-BOND BOURBON WHISKEY

The spirit must be the product of one distillation season by one distiller at one distillery. It must have been stored in a federally bonded warehouse for at least four years and bottled at 100 proof. The bottled product's label must identify the distillery where it was distilled and bottled.

Brand Example: J. T. S. Brown Kentucky Straight Bourbon Whiskey Bottled in Bond

Without definitions, however, these terms mislead consumers; they have become marketing hooks, with consumers making assumptions about what they mean. As you will learn in the coming chapters, sometimes products labeled as "small batch" do not come in small batches at all. People frequently think "sour mash" means that the bourbon is special, but it's merely a fermentation method that most distillers use.

The basic definition plainly states that bourbon needs to be made in the United States and does not provide an age requirement. A common mistake: people add American oak to the definition. As you can see, on the previous page, the government does not define the type of oak nor does it classify the type of container bourbon must be stored in. So, you could take a fresh new charred French oak bucket to the still, fill it to the top with distilled 51 percent corn mash spirit, walk it to the bottling line, pour it into a bottle, and call it bourbon. If this happened, you could taste unwanted, rotten, vegetable-like distillation notes and get a mouthful of fresh char. One day, some marketing genius will demand their distillery create one-day-old bourbon and charge $50 a bottle. Fortunately, so far, nobody is doing that.

If a brand label says "Kentucky Straight Bourbon," that means the bourbon was made in Kentucky and spent at least two years in a new charred oak container. Ubiquitous brands Woodford Reserve, Maker's Mark, and Jim Beam are all Kentucky straight bourbons, making the "minimum two years old and made in Kentucky" belief extremely common. With so many straight bourbons on the market, who can blame an enthusiast for thinking all bourbons must be at least two years old? When *straight* or only the word *bourbon* appears on the label, the producer may not add any additional flavoring. Because Canadian whiskey and some forms of Scotch allow coloring and flavoring, and because the so-called flavored whiskey category (which I detest!) confusingly uses the terms *bourbon* and *straight bourbon* on its labels, bourbons are often mistaken for having flavoring. Further adding to the confusion, in rye whiskey, the government does allow additions of coloring, flavoring, or blending materials of up to 2.5 percent by volume of the finished product. An example is Templeton Rye whiskey: the company adds a proprietary flavoring agent to the rye whiskey, but this information is not on the label, and most people don't know the additions exist in rye. The only true way to ensure you don't have flavoring in rye whiskey is to look for a label with the word *straight*, which guarantees against adulterations. In whiskey labeled *bourbon*, no coloring or flavoring is allowed. Despite these laws, there are conspiracy theorists who say brands are adding coloring or using second-use barrels to manufacture bourbon. In both cases, the distiller would face heavy fines and perhaps jail time.

The belief that all bourbon must be two years old is so pervasive that, hell, if you go on a tour at a major distillery, the tour guide might even goof and repeat this fallacy. No matter how much bourbon education reaches the mainstream, this mistake will happen.

One of the rarer labels is "bottled-in-bond" bourbon. This designation stems from congressional legislation in 1897 and was created in response to rectifiers adding prune juice, water, and even kerosene to the whiskey to make it appear older and better. Only seventeen bottled-in-bond bourbons exist today, but thanks to one man, Heaven Hill bourbon ambassador Bernie Lubbers, whose personal tagline is "Stay bonded!," the label is making a small comeback. Following Heaven Hill's example, other companies are gradually adding it to their portfolios. The Bottled-in-Bond Act of 1897 was an important piece of US consumer food protection legislation and changed the way American spirits were made. In addition to bourbon, distillers made bottled-in-bond brandy, bottled-in-bond corn

Most bottled-in-bond bourbons, like T. W. Samuels, are owned by the Heaven Hill Brands. If not for Heaven Hill, this once-proud type of bourbon would likely be extinct.

"WHISKEY" VERSUS "WHISKY"

There are two ways to spell *whiskey*. The traditional American way is with an "e," versus the Scottish preference of no "e." Maker's Mark and Hudson use big-type fonts to show their preference in whiskey spellings.

If you're a grammar lover, you're likely wondering: what's the difference between whiskey and whisky?

The spelling is a matter of preference. American and Irish whiskeys generally add the "e," while Scotch, Canadian, and Japanese whiskies often don't. With that said, complicating things, many noted bourbon brands drop the "e," including Old Forester and Maker's Mark. Furthermore, the US government continues to use "whisky" without an "e" in its regulations, and historic Scottish documents use "whiskey" *with* an "e."

Despite there being no hard and fast rule, some people really take their whiskey-versus-whisky spelling seriously. Just ask the *New York Times*: When writer Eric Asimov wrote an article about Speyside malts, he used "whiskey" with an "e." Readers pelted the newspaper with comments. Wrote Graham Kent of London, "I cannot pass over the unforgivable use by a serious writer on wines and spirits of 'whiskey' to refer to Scotch whisky. . . . I am afraid I found the constant misspelling of the product made your article quite unreadable. It is exactly the same as if you had called it 'gin' all the way through or were to describe Lafite as Burgundy. It is simply a basic error that a reputable writer should not make."

At the risk of incurring similar wrath, I will continue to use "whiskey" throughout this book.

whiskey, and bonded wines. These products became the staple of quality. If not for Heaven Hill and Lubbers, these bourbons might have been on their way to extinction, as most modern distillers do not see the benefit of a bottled-in-bond product. At a public hearing for Diageo's $115 million Shelby County, Kentucky, distillery plans in 2014, Guy Smith, a Diageo exec, laughed at me when I asked if they planned bottled-in-bond bourbons. "Why would we do that?" he asked.

Another important aspect of a bourbon label is the age statement. Some bourbons have age statements; some do not. Distilleries are required to put an age on the bottle only if the bourbon is under four years old. When there is a statement on the label, the bourbon's youngest barrel used must be the age. In other words, if a distiller mingles a ten-year-old barrel of bourbon with a six-year-old bourbon, it must label the bottle "six-year-old bourbon." The US government also states that while age may be understated, it may not be overstated. For example, fifty-nine-month-old whiskey cannot be labeled as "five years old," but it can be understated as "four years old."

In addition to the aforementioned terms, you will also find brand histories on bourbon labels, jockeying for space with terms like *smooth*, *mellow*, and *rich*. Brands will say they're the best bourbon in the world, or the label might show a medal that gives the impression that this bourbon is, in fact, the best in the world. This is all marketing smoke and mirrors, and the wording dates back to the earliest bourbon advertisements. Consumers have always responded to *smooth* and *mellow*. They sound good, right?

My goal with this book is to show you the differences between marketing and what's inside the bottle. The aforementioned regulations only offer a glimpse of what the sweet nectar might taste like. If you see "straight bourbon" on a label, you can form a taste expectation that varies from fruity and complex to woody and burning. Throw in the marketing on the label, and you're stuck picking out bourbons based on copywriting. Don't get me wrong, marketing is extremely important to the whiskey maker, and sometimes to the drinker, but there's only so much on the label you can verify. The best way to find whiskey you like is to drink it!

We are living in perhaps the most exciting time in bourbon history, both from a business perspective and because of the wealth of consumer options.

IS JACK DANIEL'S BOURBON?

A common question for whiskey experts is, Jack Daniel's—is that a bourbon? The answer is both yes and no.

Prior to Prohibition, the government listed Jack Daniel's as bourbon even though it was known as Tennessee whiskey, which used a charcoal-filtering process known as the Lincoln County Process. In 1944, Lem Motlow (Jack Daniel's nephew and successor) received special designation from the Treasury Agency to call Jack Daniel's Tennessee whiskey. The government said this charcoal mellowing process did not exist elsewhere and that "Jack Daniel's is officially designated as a Tennessee Whiskey."

Interestingly, early 1900s bourbon producers also subscribed to charcoal-filtering pre-aged bourbon. At the Filson Historical Society, the Beall-Booth family correspondence indicates the family's distillers filtered their distilled spirit with "about 18 to 20 inches thick of pulverized charcoal made of good green wood such as sugar tree hickory." Thus, the government was likely a little harsh on Motlow's efforts. Nonetheless, Jack Daniel's began marketing itself as Tennessee whiskey and never looked back.

But there is no federal definition for Tennessee whiskey, confusing treaty writers and bars around the world. In the North American Free Trade Agreement, Tennessee whiskey is defined as: "straight Bourbon Whiskey authorized to be produced only in the State of Tennessee." Other free trade agreements carry similar language, opening the case for Jack Daniel's to be considered a bourbon. Then the door was slightly shut in 2013, when Tennessee lawmakers passed a bill that defined its state's whiskey.

State of Tennessee House Bill No. 1084 signed May 13, 2013, by Governor Bill Haslam

An intoxicating liquor may not be advertised, described, labeled, named, sold, or referred to for marketing or sales purposes as "Tennessee Whiskey," "Tennessee Whisky," "Tennessee Sour Mash Whiskey," or "Tennessee Sour Mash Whisky" unless the intoxicating liquor is:

(1) Manufactured in Tennessee;
(2) Made of a grain mixture that is at least fifty-one percent (51%) corn;
(3) Distilled to no more than 160 proof or eighty percent (80%) alcohol by volume;
(4) Aged in new, charred oak barrels in Tennessee;
(5) Filtered through maple charcoal prior to aging;
(6) Placed in the barrel at no more than 125 proof or sixty-two and one-half percent (62.5 %) alcohol by volume; and
(7) Bottled at not less than 80 proof or forty percent (40%) alcohol by volume.

A year later, the biggest competitor of Jack Daniel's, Diageo (parent company of George Dickel Tennessee Whisky), pursued the repeal of the Tennessee whiskey definition, allowing distillers to age whiskey in used barrels. Diageo failed to win a repeal of the law. It then sued the state over the 1937 law that required Tennessee spirits be aged in Tennessee. Diageo lost this bid, too, and made quite a few enemies in the American whiskey world.

As it stands today, Tennessee whiskey is still essentially bourbon that's aged in Tennessee and filtered through maple charcoal prior to aging. But you won't hear people in Tennessee calling Tennessee whiskey "bourbon," and to most bourbon lovers, *Jack Daniel's* is a dirty word.

CHAPTER ONE

BOURBON
POLITICS

When I interviewed Tom Bulleit in 2008, the Bulleit Bourbon founder told me something that forever changed the way I taste and write about bourbon. Bulleit sank into his Victorian chair and said, "Bourbon is a lot less about what's inside the bottle and a lot more about what you tell people." He called this the art of suggestion, pointing toward his ear, and continued by saying that marketing essentially commands the bourbon industry. Bulleit's assessment was correct. The labels, stories, and even books about bourbon are greatly influenced by the publicists and marketers who represent the brands. They are the keepers of the history—and with so few of us trying to offer something other than these brand stories, the marketer's narrative tends to own the marketplace of bourbon thought.

Bulleit's art of suggestion, as he calls it, really begins as folklore in the 1700s. It grows to legendary status in the 1800s, becomes reported fact in the 1900s, and comes to irritate consumers in the 2000s.

The proof, age, and whiskey type are about the only things you can trust on an American whiskey label. Bourbon labels rival political ads for the most bullshit per square inch.

BOURBON AND LAWSUITS

It might surprise you to learn that when master distillers congregate, they actually get along. In fact, distillers brag about how the camaraderie is passed down from one generation to another. They enjoy a rare bond unfound in many alcohol industries.

As for the marketing and sales people, well, that's a different story. They typically can't stand the presence of their competitors and have a history of suing one another. In fact, you could say suing their competitors is a rite of passage for whiskey distillers. Bourbon icons E. H. Taylor and George T. Stagg sued each other's companies in the 1800s; today, Buffalo Trace makes brands named after both men. Brown-Forman, parent company of Jack Daniel's, sued the brand Ezra Brooks over label confusion in the 1960s and lost. Nearly fifty years later, Brown-Forman sued Barton Brands to protect another brand, Woodford Reserve, and won.

They sue over campaigns. In 2011, Wild Turkey and Old Crow were entangled in litigation over the phrase "Give 'Em the Bird." The Kentucky Distillers' Association (KDA), a trade group for Kentucky distillers, sued Buffalo Trace for using its trademarks, specifically "Kentucky Bourbon Trail," as well as similar logos. Buffalo Trace is not a KDA member.

They sue the little guys, too. When a company comes out with a wax seal on its liquor bottle top, Maker's Mark lawyers send letters to make sure the wax doesn't drip down like it does on that brand's bottles, which federal courts upheld as a Maker's Mark trademark in *Maker's Mark Distillery, Inc. v. Diageo North America, Inc.* Should the wax drip, it's lawsuit time. Sazerac, which owns Buffalo Trace, sued Bison Ridge Distillery in Minnesota for adopting a similar name and packaging.

But the worst lawsuit of them all, and perhaps an indication that legal measures are in bourbon blood, was this one: James E. Pepper sued his mother, Nanna, for control of the Oscar Pepper Distillery when Oscar passed away in 1865. Nobody is safe.

Michter's Distillery tells its consumers that George Washington once served its whiskey to his troops—an impossibility, as Michter's didn't exist in the late 1700s. But the original Michter's Distillery was in

MICHTER'S
ORIGINAL POT STILL SOUR MASH
WHISKEY

DISTILLED AND BOTTLED BY MICHTER'S JUG HOUSE, SCHAEFFERSTOWN, PA.

AMERICA'S OLDEST DISTILLERY
ESTABLISHED 1753

Michter's is a historic brand with deep roots in bourbon legend. The original distillery owners claimed the site once served George Washington's troops. The brand went bankrupt in the late 1980s; it's now owned by Chatham Imports and is operating in Kentucky with the similar label.

Schaefferstown, Pennsylvania, owned by distiller John Shenk in 1753. The property boasted two of Lebanon County's twenty stills and was just a farm distillery, like every other one in the area. General Washington was known to purchase whiskey from this area for his soldiers. In the 1970s, Michter's owner Louis Forman exploited this faint connection, calling the newly named Michter's "America's Oldest Distillery" and craftily marketing it as George Washington's beverage of choice for the health of his men—and by extension, the American nation. Fast-forward to the 1990s, after Forman's company went out of business and Chatham Imports acquired Michter's abandoned trademarks. Michter's new website contained the same Washington story, only this time, the whiskey came from Kentucky instead of Pennsylvania. Michter's became one of the many whiskey brands that purchased whiskey from other distilleries and bottled it themselves. However, some drinkers questioned the ethical practice of using the Washington story, since the whiskey was no longer coming from the same distillery. "The Washington story is a part of the brand's history," says Joe Magglioco, Michter's president. And so, despite heavy criticism from a minority group of consumers (who frequently bombard Michter's social media feeds with derogatory comments, calling Michter's "scum" and "frauds"), the brand keeps its founding legend alive.

Another legendary marketing loophole lies with Elijah Craig, a brand named after a Baptist minister who was originally credited for inventing bourbon. The real-life minister is commonly referred to as the Father of Bourbon, but a 1970s whiskey scholar disputed this.[1] We can all appreciate the fact that records proving Craig's distilling capabilities might be lost—damn Google for not existing then!—but the legend actually revolves around his discovering the charred-barrel technique after a barn fire magically charred the insides of his barrels. Let's think about this one for a second. How the hell is a fire burning the inside of a barrel but leaving the outside untouched? Perhaps Craig survived the only fire in history that selected what it burned. "Immaculate charception."

Heaven Hill, the owners of Elijah Craig bourbons, admit they use this story tongue-in-cheek, and former Maker's Mark CEO Bill Samuels told me that the industry needed to crown an "inventor" to help its marketing in the early days. Long before Heaven Hill

continued on page 24

PRESIDENTS AND WHISKEY

US presidents and whiskey have a long history together.

It all begins with the country's first president. **George Washington**'s Mount Vernon Distillery operated five copper-pot stills that produced nearly eleven thousand gallons of whiskey in 1799. His distiller, a Scot named James Anderson, distilled a 60 percent rye, 35 percent corn, and 5 percent malted barley mashbill, as well as brandy and cinnamon whiskey.

Washington operated one of the largest distilleries in the country, but he was certainly not the first distiller. Of course, as a general, he purchased whiskey from Pennsylvania whiskey makers, who later revolted against

Library of Congress

Washington's government when the United States enacted an alcohol tax.

To pay its war debts, the country decided to tax whiskey makers. More than four hundred revolted against the government and refused to pay. So-called whiskey rebels attacked Pittsburgh's John Neville, a pesky tax collector, and Washington federalized 12,950 troops to thwart western Pennsylvania distillers' efforts. From 1791 to 1794, the new United States of America wasn't so united, and the conflict was all about taxing whiskey. The matter was eventually resolved, but not before many distillers joined other whiskey makers in Kentucky.

Washington wasn't the only American president involved with a whiskey scandal. President **Ulysses Grant** was caught up in the great Whiskey Ring, one of the biggest political corruption scandals of the 1800s.

Frequently accused of being a drunk, Grant loved whiskey. In particular, he enjoyed the taste of Old Crow, one of the early brand names. Whiskey makers also apparently loved Grant. Perhaps the president's whiskey consumption was good for business? Several distilleries conspired to defraud the government of taxes and used these funds to finance the Republican Party's national campaign for the reelection of President Grant.

In 1875, federal agents raided distilleries in Saint Louis, Cincinnati, Milwaukee, and Chicago, seizing illicit whiskey and records, and arrested the owners and indicted Grant's general and friend, Orville E. Babcock.

Since these distillers had defrauded the country of more than $3 million— $1.2 million of which was unaccounted for—and since Babcock was Grant's close associate, the country demanded to know just how involved, if at all, the president was in the scandal. Much like President **Richard Nixon**'s Watergate scandal, Americans wondered just how much Grant really knew.

Grant swore that when he first learned of the Whiskey Ring, he told his staff to fully investigate it. Then, it was discovered that Babcock was involved, and Grant offered strong testimony in defense of his general's character. Thanks to the president's testimony, Babcock was acquitted, but 240 distillers, government officials, and go-betweens were indicted. Only 110 were found guilty, but most of these went to jail.

Grant's testimony is the only occasion a standing US president has ever testified in a criminal case, and because of this it is the conspiracy theorist's strongest evidence that he was involved. Why else would he offer such praise to a man suspected of cheating the government?

If this scandal happened today, you might see a few Grant whiskey labels coming to the market. But the scandal was just too fresh and sharp for contemporaries to lead to any humorous brands. The only Grant whiskey label that came from this ordeal was Jos. P. Spang & Co.'s Grant 63 Whiskey, launched around 1892. Grant 63 used the president's likeness to market its "perfect whiskey," but Grant himself didn't live to taste it, having died in 1885.

Despite Old Crow using the president's product preference in its marketing materials, the lack of a Whiskey Ring or President Grant brand just goes to show that bourbon companies may prefer to market legends over truths. One of the great cases in point is Jefferson's Bourbon, named after President Thomas Jefferson. In a letter to Colonel Charles Yancey, regarding a man's petition to start a brewery, Jefferson wrote, "I wish to see this beverage become common instead of whiskey, which kills one-third of our citizens and ruins their families."[2] Jefferson didn't hold whiskey protests or seek a prohibition against whiskey, but he obviously didn't care for it. Chet Zoeller, the cofounder of Jefferson's Bourbon, told me they just wanted a recognizable name on their label to move product. And it is a fact that Jefferson was the president who repealed the whiskey tax. But wouldn't a President Grant whiskey with a true story be more interesting? Well, maybe not. Given the country's low test scores and man-on-the-street interviews in which twenty-somethings say that America went to war with the South during the Revolutionary War, many people may not even recognize Grant's name.

In bourbon circles, President William Howard Taft is actually the most beloved president. Elected into the Kentucky Distillers' Association's Bourbon Hall of Fame, Taft gave an answer to a vague question after the passing of the Pure Food and Drug Act of 1906. Blended bourbons and straight bourbons were considered whiskey under the new law. Taft provided clarity.

Published by the National Wholesale Liquor Dealers Association on December 27, 1909, the president's nine-page answer to the question "What is whiskey?" forever protected straight bourbon whiskey from containing grain neutral spirits or being confused with blended bourbons. "The public will be made to know exactly the kind of whiskey they buy and drink. If they desire straight whiskey, they can secure it by purchasing what is branded 'straight whiskey.' If they are willing to drink whiskey made from neutral spirits, then, they can buy it under a brand showing it; and if they are content with a blend of flavors made by the mixture of straight whiskey and whiskey made from neutral spirits, the brand of the blend upon the package will enable them to buy and drink that which they desire," President Taft wrote.

Taft's clarification of whiskey became law, and today's government regulations for whiskey are essentially Taft's words with a couple of additions. In 1938, "aged in new barrels" was added to the regulation and "manufactured only in the United States" was added in 1964.

Without Taft laying down the law, we might still be drinking bourbons with grain neutral spirits.

continued from page 20

established the Elijah Craig brand in 1986, the bourbon industry was carrying on the minister's legend, likely to stick it to the Woman's Christian Temperance Union, which influenced Prohibition. You can't help but chuckle about a Baptist preacher making bourbon, when several Protestant Christian denominations, including his own, frowned upon drinking.

Despite Heaven Hill removing the legend from its label, the Elijah Craig story still appears from time to time in legitimate magazines and newspapers. At the end of the day, it's only whiskey, and the *New York Times* lifestyle editor isn't hiring a freelance fact checker to verify bourbon's origins.

Do people really care about legends influencing the historic truths? Some do, and some don't.

There's a faction of whiskey drinkers known as whiskey geeks. These people belong to a few secret bourbon societies. (Yes, there are actual secret bourbon societies in the cyber webs of Facebook and the dusty basements of bars.) Bourbon is their love, their hobby and, for many, the reason why they wake up in the morning. They are lawyers, doctors, pilots, janitors, and people from many other walks of life. They take bourbon so seriously that they report distillers to the federal government for mislabeling products. These people heckle companies for any advertisement that misrepresents the whiskey truth, and they live to correct the Mr. Bourbon Know-Nothing who breathes fumes at you at the bar and tries to force his ignorance cloaked as knowledge on the public. I am a whiskey geek, and we are a passionate people who've become the de facto Whiskey Police, keeping brands in check in social media. We have become so powerful that some American whiskey brands pursue the geeks' opinions in public forums. But we still represent a minority of the whiskey consumer base, and some brands just don't care what we think.

Members of the larger audience walk into a liquor store, pick up a bottle, and are intrigued with the label. They buy the product, drink it, and either like the whiskey or don't. This audience is becoming affluent with its bourbon knowledge and is eager to learn more, but they do not immediately accept the aforementioned whiskey geeks' policy of truth in labeling. In the beginning, these new consumers just want good whiskey. Then, they really start falling in love with particular brands

MGP Ingredients is a conglomerate food and agricultural company that owns and operates a former Seagram's distillery in Lawrenceburg, Indiana. It contract distills or provides sourced whiskey to many distilleries and bottlers. Many of its clients have failed to disclose their whiskey source and endured public scrutiny or lawsuits.

and their backstories, and when they sometimes learn that a backstory is hyperbole, they either accept the half truths or blanket lies or they feel outright deceived.

Whiskey geeks frequently target Michter's for their belief that the Pennsylvania legacy is a misrepresentation of the whiskey inside the bottle. But the parent company of Michter's purchased the brand's namesake when nobody else wanted it. That means they own the rights to the Michter's name; should they not be allowed to market the original brand's legacy? Another example is Templeton Rye Whiskey. Templeton, Iowa, is a small town that made a ton of illicit whiskey during Prohibition, even supplying Al Capone for his bootlegging operation. In the mid-2000s, a tan tin-sided building appeared on the main drag of Templeton with a few barrels out front and a tiny still inside. Shortly after this building was erected, Templeton aged rye whiskey started appearing on the store shelf. How was this possible? They'd just opened their doors and already had a well-aged whiskey? Was it magic? Nope. They purchased bulk whiskey from a former Seagram's distillery in Lawrenceburg, Indiana, that was selling all of its whiskey to anybody and everybody just to keep the lights on. The Indiana distillery changed owners a few times, and the plant was nearly shut down, until its former parent company, CL Financial, developed the business model of selling aged whiskey to start-up companies like Templeton.

Templeton slapped the town's true Prohibition story on its back label, and people fell in love with the whiskey. But when the truth was revealed—that the whiskey hadn't really been made in Iowa—people were pissed off, and Templeton faced three class-action lawsuits under consumer protection laws.

This sort of thing is hardly new. Since whiskey companies have been in business, distillers have worked with other distillers or independent bottlers to provide whiskey for another company's product. Today, these independent bottlers are called non-distiller producers (NDPs), a term coined by Bourbon Hall of Famer and whiskey writer Chuck Cowdery. NDPs are companies that do not own their own distilleries and instead purchase whiskey from somebody else. The whiskey geeks don't mind the so-called NDPs; they just seem to get irritated with the backstories. Back in the 1940s and 1960s, the Stitzel-Weller Distillery was providing whiskey to the Old Medley Distillery and contract distilling for Austin, Nichols, and Company, while Glenmore Distillery sold hundreds of barrels to bottlers needing supply. The bottlers slapped their pretty labels on somebody else's whiskey, they sold it to consumers who were happy to drink it, and nobody felt deceived. That was the business.

Back then, however, the Internet didn't exist. Special bourbon forums, such as StraightBourbon.com, and other social media sites have given enthusiasts platforms to share information about recipes, water, distillation techniques, and history. Back in the old days, consumers didn't have access to much of this information, and distillers could get away with changing a recipe. It's more difficult for bourbon makers to get away with stretching the truth today.

When Maker's Mark watered down its bourbon whiskey to "meet demand" in February 2013, for example, the general American public called the iconic whiskey brand greedy, and international social media blew up with pure rage. Core fans reminded Maker's Mark that they once promised that they would never change their product. But they did change it, lowering the alcohol proof from 90 to 84, and fans spoke. "You BASTARDS!!!! I love Maker's! But I'm going to switch! Hope you're happy!! Because I'm pissed," wrote fan Tony Aguilar on the Facebook announcement.

The online outrage pushed the Maker's Mark proof-lowering story to front-page news, prime-time TV's lead, and the butt of jokes on late-night talk shows. All the while, brand fans felt betrayed and simply wanted to know why. Within eight days of lowering its proof, Maker's Mark reversed its decision and enjoyed another week of prime-time coverage. Had the original move been a publicity stunt or just bad management?

We'll likely never know, because Maker's Mark and its parent company, Beam Suntory, treat the "proof debacle" (as they call it) like a hardened combat veteran treats the war: they just don't talk about it. But it's important to note that lowering proof helps stretch the product into more bottles, and fictitious backstories intrigue new consumers. Both have been going on since American whiskey became profit minded.

The whiskey business is not an altruistic industry run by choirboys. Distillers don't take oaths of purity or do what's in the best interest of their consumers. They do what they do to make money, and hyperbole and today's marketing liberties are a part of this industry's history. Bourbon folklore draws us in like Greek mythology, hooking us and making us interested in learning more. The fact that much of the spirit's history is based on legends just makes for a better story, and it spices up the truth for a drinking culture that passionately wants information now—right or wrong.

There is no greater example of this than the Craig legend, which credits the minister with inventing bourbon around 1794.

The fact is, the term *bourbon* first appeared in print in 1821 in Bourbon County's *Western Citizen* newspaper, where the Stout and Adams advertising firm promoted "bourbon whiskey by the barrel or keg." Five years later, a Lexington, Kentucky, grocer wrote to distiller John Corlis to order more whiskey from "barrels burnt upon the inside, say only a 16th of an inch."[3] This is the earliest known reference of charring the insides of barrels in reference to whiskey.

But in all likelihood, distillers were charring barrels and using bourbon mashbills long before those references. In 1809's *The Practical Distiller*, author Samuel M'Harry of Lancaster County, Pennsylvania, suggests burning the inside of barrels to clean them and offers a whiskey grain recipe of two-thirds corn and one-third rye. M'Harry was quite fond of corn. "That corn has as much and as good whiskey as rye or any other grain. . . . Corn is always from one to two shillings per bushel cheaper than rye, and in many places much plentier." If he had suggested this recipe be placed in a new charred oak barrel, he would have published a bourbon whiskey recipe.

Early Americans distilled whatever they could. In areas where grapes and other fruits were plentiful, they made brandy. In the New England area, they distilled molasses to create rum. Corn and rye were far cheaper and more plentiful than molasses and fruits, so that's why these grains became the cornerstone for early American distillations. People love giving romantic stories about corn waving in the breeze and rye brushing against the distiller's cheek, claiming that's why corn became bourbon's backbone, but that's just a bunch of baloney. Much

PINECONE LIKKER

Is pinecone liquor real? Sort of.

In the popular adult cartoon *Squidbillies*, the main character, Early Cuyler, earns his living selling pinecone-infused spirits and other intoxicants. But this is not the only reference to a pinecone spirit.

Of the many treatments for tuberculosis, pinecone-infused "likker" (as it was colloquially known to the moonshiners who made it) offered curative properties. Doctors of Oriental medicine later determined it was likely the pinecone that offered healing, not the spirits, and further study led researchers to discover pinecones were rich in Vitamin C. During World War II, with orange shortages, Vitamin C–deficient Russian soldiers were given pine needle–infused vodka. Today, Austria is the world leader in pinecone liquor, promoting its pinecone-flavored schnapps, *Zirbenschnaps*.

THE SOUR-MASH RECIPE

When you see *sour mash* or *original sour mash* on a bourbon label, you're getting a spoonful of marketing. Everybody uses the sour-mash fermentation technique, and the constant use of "sour mash" on labeling is a little like a car manufacturer saying its model uses unleaded gasoline. But for whatever reason, became a strong buzzword in whiskey labeling, so you'll find it plastered all over.

The sour-mash fermentation process is when the distiller takes about a quarter of an already fermented mash (looking like hot cereal) and adds it to the new mash set for fermentation. The distillers call this the "backset" because the previous mash has been held back from the first distillation run. The backset keeps wild yeast from invading the new mash and decreases the chances of bacterial infestations. If distillers don't do this, the wild yeast, which live all around us, can ruin the mash and make inconsistent whiskey. A Scottish doctor named James C. Crow is credited with industrializing this technique for distillers, but the first known sour-mash recipe belongs to a woman—Catherine Frye Spears Carpenter. In 1818, the Catherine Carpenter Distillery gave instructions on how to make sour-mash whiskey:

> Put into the mash tub six bushels of very hot soup then put in one bushel of corn meal ground pretty coarse. Stir well, then sprinkle a little meal over the mash. Let it stand five days—that is three full days betwixt the day you mash and the day you cool off—on the fifth day put in three gallons of warm water. Then, put in one gallon of rye meal and one gallon of malt to work it well into the malt and stir for three quarters of an hour. Then, fill the tub half full of luke warm water. Stir it well and with a fine sieve or otherwise break all the lumps fine. Then, let it stand three hours. . . . Fill up the tub with luke warm water."

as the barrel-charring legend of Elijah Craig originated somewhere, the common legend about why distillers came to prefer corn is usually linked to the Corn Patch and Cabin Rights Act of 1776.

When Kentucky was still a part of Virginia, Virginians migrated there to raise the population in the soon-to-be state, as well as for land speculation. The Virginia legislature attempted to "regularize" Western lands and came up with the Corn Patch and Cabin Rights law, which allowed settlers to claim land if they built a cabin and planted corn in sections of Kentucky prior to January 1, 1778. But in their infinite wisdom, Virginia lawmakers failed to specify the cabin or corn patch size. Settlers planted three or four seeds of corn and built a small cabin with a few pieces of lumber, expecting to receive land. Thus, while it's possible the Corn Patch and Cabin Rights Act helped a few distilling families establish themselves, the law was so "clumsy" and "unwork-able"[4] that it is likely to have had little impact at all on bourbon.

People distilled what they could to survive, trade, and get drunk. It's really that simple. If settlers had found nothing but pinecones, there's a good chance "America's spirit" would be pinecone liquor, an ode to a summer breeze wafting through the towering pine trees.

Fortunately, corn, rye, and barley were harvested for whiskey, and distillers never toyed around with pinecone liquor. Or it never took off, anyway.

In times of corn overproduction, distilling the grain became a profitable venture for farmers and an eventual necessary savior to sagging grain prices. Although corn prices have fluctuated throughout American history, farmers know it's a tried-and-true fact that people drink in good and bad economies. And that's the real reason corn became the base of bourbon's recipe: it grew.

WHO MADE THE FIRST BOURBON?

I believe some early Americans actually made what would qualify as bourbon but called it "corn brandy." My friend and bourbon historian Mike Veach maintains an incredible bourbon collection for the Filson Historical Society, and in the diaries of two Frenchmen, brothers John and Louis Tarascon, Veach learned the brothers rectified white whiskey and sold it as corn brandy. It's likely the Tarascons, who grew up near the Cognac region, brought the French brandy technique of charring barrels to whiskey aging. It's certainly possible that they were also referring to the Swedish production of "corn brandy," which was a spirit of mashed grain intentionally not completely rectified and diluted with water. Nineteenth-century connoisseurs said Swedish corn brandy was the "nearest approach" to making whiskey but was inferior.[5] But given the fact that the Swedes' version was largely isolated to their own region, it's more plausible that the Frenchmen applied their country's barrel-charring techniques and called the distilled spirit aged in barrels corn brandy. Brandy was what the French made, so they just aptly named the distilled corn spirit such. During the time, booze names were not as defined as they are today. There's a good chance distilled potatoes were called whiskey, and people who thought they were drinking whiskey were really drinking vodka. Besides, most early American spirits were rectified to enhance the color. Rectifying meant adding prune juice, tobacco spit, rattlesnake heads and turpentine—you know, stuff that's gross and will kill you—to make a clear spirit look more like aged whiskey.

Adding to the argument that the barrel-charring technique was created by the French, I've found bourbon's aromatics to be similar to cognac's nose, whereas bourbon and Scotch offer little to no taste or smell similarities. And bourbon whiskey is almost certainly named after a Frenchman. Well, kind of.

The two going theories about bourbon's namesake are that it's either named after Bourbon County in Kentucky or Bourbon Street in New Orleans. Both places were named after the Bourbons, the longtime ruling family of France. If you buy the Bourbon County theory, then you believe that early New Orleans merchants enjoyed the whiskey from barrels stamped "Limestone, Bourbon County, Kentucky." Like the Craig legend, however, this one falls apart when you really analyze it: shipments from Kentucky to New Orleans took a year, and Veach writes, it is "therefore unlikely that there were enough whiskey shipments invoiced to Limestone to catch the attention of New Orleanians."[6] He suggests river travelers may have drunk aged whiskey on New Orleans' Bourbon Street, and that's where bourbon earned its name.

But the sad truth is we'll likely never definitively know who truly invented bourbon or why he or she named it so.

Bourbon does not enjoy the centuries' worth of historical research that beer and wine have commanded. Universities are only now taking bourbon history seriously, and the distilleries closely guard their true histories. Distillers owned slaves, ran whiskey during Prohibition, and used prostitutes for their marketing, and many of these connections still haunt bourbon's ruling families. The Pogue family, for example, sold barrels to Cincinnati bootlegger George Remus during Prohibition. "Not a proud moment in our history, but some really neat history nonetheless," Paul Pogue told me. That's why legends and misnomers have permeated bourbon culture; the truth isn't always pretty, and it certainly won't sell whiskey. In fact, I surmise that early bourbon marketers promoted Elijah Craig and other legends to hide the unscrupulous truth.

For as long as traders have hitched their whiskey-filled wagons and tried to outsell the other guy, whiskey has been smack in the middle of unethical practices. Today's folklore labels pale in comparison to the 1800s-era whiskey salesmen, who showed absolutely no signs of decency.

Many believe whiskey started the war between Native American tribes and the United States government. Whiskey traders took advantage of the tribes. In this drawing, published by Frank Leslie's illustrated newspaper on February 3, 1872, Indians try to drink contraband whiskey destroyed by authorities. *Library of Congress*

WHISKEY ON THE PLAINS—A PARTY OF INDIANS, DISCO

EARLY WHISKEY SALESMEN

When the United States was founded, settlers built relationships with Native American tribes, trading goods for fur pelts. You'll find no shortage of literature condemning how this country acquired land from Indians. And right smack in the middle of this land grab was whiskey.

Settlers treasured furs, using them for shelter, wagons, clothing, and containers. Moreover, the huge international demand for beaver hats meant that furs were big business in the early modern global economy. Indians were at the center of this trade, as they essentially cornered the

T OF CONTRABAND WHISKY IS BEING DESTROYED BY THE AUTHORITIES, ENDEAVOR TO SAVE WHAT THEY CAN.
A SKETCH BY OUR SPECIAL ARTIST.—SEE PAGE 334.

market on pelts by being the experts in their harvest. They, like all other peoples, developed a taste for whiskey. Traders took advantage of this desire for distilled spirits, getting their Native partners drunk and either trading for pelts far below their value or outright stealing them while the Indian traders were intoxicated. These whiskey traders often became the first white men that tribal leaders dealt with, and the traders sought to secure their influence with individual leaders as well as whole villages. "Each trader endeavors to impress the Indians with a belief that all other traders have no object but to cheat and deceive them, and that government intends taking away their lands by sending troops into their country," wrote Colonel H. Atkinson, the commanding officer of the 6th Infantry Regiment, in 1819. "Hence the jealousy and distrust of the Indians towards government, and the bad opinion they have of whites for truth and honesty."[7]

Whiskey crippled Indian nations, rendering them useless for hunts. It increased violence and often brought forth an unquenchable addiction that destroyed many lives.

Many agreed with Atkinson's sentiment, arguing that early American whiskey traders destroyed potential peace talks with tribes. Colonel Clark W. Thompson, onetime superintendent of Indian Affairs in Saint Paul, Minnesota, believed the bloody war between the Sioux and United States began over whiskey. "I have made many and varied efforts to stop the sale of whiskey to the Indians. . . . The whiskey traffic is a great drawback to the welfare of Indians," Thompson testified before Congress in 1862. "In my opinion, the whole Sioux nation was suddenly precipitated into a war with us through the influence of a little whiskey upon the brains of four Indians, for there is no evidence to show that it was a premeditated move."[8]

By the 1880s, whiskey was both a tribal and a national epidemic, arguably started by unsavory traders looking to cheat Native Americans. The US government publicly blamed the whiskey trader as much as possible, perhaps to shield its own whiskey-distribution efforts and its removal and massacring of Native groups. Nonetheless, unethical white men were among the country's first whiskey marketers. "These whiskey traffickers . . . seem to be void of all conscience, rob and murder many of the Indians," wrote Richard W. Cummins, an Indian agent. "They will get them drunk, and then take their horses, guns or blankets off their backs, regardless of how quick they may freeze to death." Cummins also called the trader "a dishonest man—a man that will condescend to the meanest of acts."

They didn't even have the decency to give Indians the good stuff. So-called Indian whiskey was defined as "Whiskey adulterated for sale to the Indians."[9] Traders added foul ingredients to whiskey sold to the tribes—in the Ozark Mountains of Arkansas, they made a special whiskey for Natives called the Redskin White Mule because of its destructive powers.

The shameful history of the whiskey traders illustrates why legends, not truth, became important in the marketing of bourbon. A historically accurate Indian whiskey-trader bourbon brand would be considered both racist and distasteful, and it would probably face boycotts, poor sales, and perhaps even failure.

Moreover, whiskey makers were often slave owners, which would also be problematic on a marketing label. Even President Thomas Jefferson worked with a contract distiller to make whiskey for his slaves, and President George Washington used seven slave distillers at his distillery. If a slave had "distiller" listed as one of his skills, plantation owners would spend top dollar to acquire him. In the despicable 1826–1827 slave catalogue *Slave Trade: Slaves Imported, Exported*, the author describes an unnamed slave as "a very well behaved man; a good distiller and a generally useful sort of person." He then describes another man, who "was beaten by the driver" and "work[ed] as a distiller half the year."[10]

Slavery is a conversation we tend to avoid as a nation; in whiskey, it's a conversation distillers pray never comes up. At the Catherine Spears Frye Carpenter Distillery, whose 1818 recipe book contains the first known sour-mash whiskey recipe, the family owned several slaves, ranging in value and listed in the family's account books as "taxable property."

The fact is, bourbon is mostly made in Kentucky, and prior to the Civil War the Bluegrass State was a major slave state. The famous distiller E. H. Taylor was the son of a major slave trader. When Kentucky became a state in 1792, 23 percent of the state's households kept slaves.[11]

Slavery is this country's burden to bear, and early whiskey makers took part in this shameful act. Just like an Indian-trader whiskey label, you will not find slave whiskey labels anytime soon, but like Indians, slaves are very much a part of early American whiskey. Slaves' full contributions to American whiskey may never be known, but I surmise they created many of this country's first whiskeys. The fact that slave-selling guides placed a premium on distillation as a skill shows that slave distillers were obviously highly sought after; it's a shame we'll never know their true part in the development of bourbon. Yet in every bourbon legend, the mention of slavery is conspicuously absent.

You will, however, find modern whiskey labels celebrating a felony sport. American whiskey and cockfighting, the bloody death match between two roosters, have long had a strong connection. Both grew in popularity in the 1800s. Watching two roosters disembowel one another was considered one heckuva a good time, and this led to early American whiskey companies both depicting cockfighting in their advertisements and naming brands after famous cocks. The use of cocks in a whiskey brand was so popular that start-up brands tried to imitate successful ones. In the late 1800s, US courts determined that the name of Miller's Game Cock Whiskey infringed upon the trademark of a separately owned Miller's Chicken Cock Whiskey. The landmark case said the use of "Chicken" instead of "Game" created confusion.

Today, cock labels confuse nobody and incite chuckles for their innuendo. When contemporary labels Chicken Cock Whiskey and One Foot Cock Whiskey were launched in recent years, frat boys everywhere ran to the liquor stores and purchased them for gag gifts and laughs. But those two whiskeys are barely worthy of a fraternity's toilet bowl. On the other hand, Fighting Cock Kentucky Straight Bourbon Whiskey is one of the greatest values in all of whiskey. The six-year-old bourbon label depicts a rooster in full attack mode, its razor-sharp talons prepared to slice open its unlucky foe.

Cockfighting holds a strong tradition in whiskey-making areas, and I imagine there are still quite a few illegal cockfighting rings in illicit moonshine country. But this particular label likely appeals to old-school farmers. I certainly cannot see an animal rights activist buying Fighting Cock. No group has made a large-scale attack about its label or meaning, but bourbon is generally trying to move away from this hillbilly and farmer look in an effort to appeal to younger, city-dwelling folk. Cock labels will remain a novelty.

What will never go away in American whiskey is the rectifier, a dirty word in many circles, who mixes distillations or aged whiskey with various compounds. Many famous whiskey names operated under rectifier licenses: George Garvin Brown, founder of Brown-Forman, and brand namesake W. L. Weller were both rectifiers. In the 1800s, rectifier companies largely owned the bourbon market and operated in downtown Louisville, Kentucky, on a strip called "Whiskey Row." They purchased bourbon whiskey from distillers and blended the bourbon with clear grain spirits and added coloring. In 1896, a congressional committee concluded that distillers sold the majority of straight bourbon to rectifiers instead of consumers.[12] In turn, the rectifiers diluted the straight whiskey and sold it.

All the while, in the 1800s, taverns and saloons purchased barrels of whiskey direct from the wholesaler. Much like the rectifiers, the tavern owners wanted to earn a lofty profit, so they added a few choice ingredients to the barrel of whiskey to make it last longer. For some reason, tobacco juice was a prime additive. Perhaps it added decent coloring, but can you imagine ordering a shot of whiskey and half it being tobacco spit? Suffice it to say, many consumers were getting sick from bad whiskey, and the country had a serious issue on its hands—consumers needed protection.

In 1897, Congress passed the Bottled-in-Bond Act to ensure consumers received a good product. At the time, whiskey distillers typically did not bottle their own products. They sold barrels of whiskey to wholesalers, who bottled it. This act became the first piece of consumer protection legislation in American history and gave the power to the distillery companies versus the rectifiers.

These days, rectifiers are another bane of American whiskey history. The sheer thought of adding grain spirits to bourbon is enough to make aficionados like myself want to gag. But rectifier licenses still exist. Kentucky's Alcoholic Beverage Control Laws define a modern rectifier thusly: "The license authorizes the licensee to purify or refine distilled spirits and wine. The holder of a rectifier's license may purchase from distillers." Many major brands operate under rectifier licenses, including Jefferson's and Old Rip Van Winkle, because they don't own distilleries. Instead of adding caramel coloring, however, today's bourbon rectifiers mingle barrels of bourbon from the same

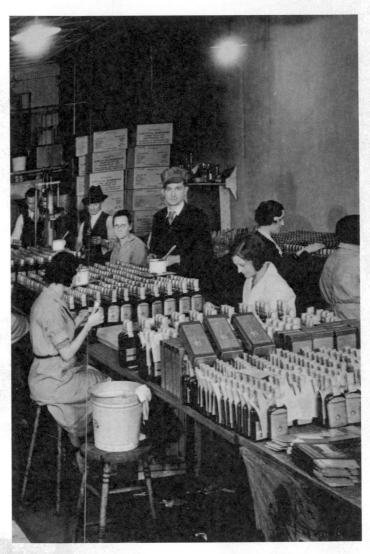

The Bottled-in-Bond Act of 1897 not only gave consumers confidence in the country's bourbon, it also gave women career opportunities. Women became the chief bottling-line operators because they were considered to be more coordinated than men and to break fewer bottles. *Oscar Getz Museum of Whiskey*

HOW TO MAKE GOLDEN WEDDING BOURBON

In Henry William Hilsebusch's 1904 book *Knowledge of a Rectifier*, he instructed readers how he made "Golden Wedding Bourbon," a once popular brand of whiskey that still appears in today's auction sales. To make the fake stuff, you simply add twenty-five gallons of "some good straight heavy bodied whiskey, rye or bourbon." Then, you add twenty gallons of "clean spirits, double distilled, known to the trade as French or Daisy spirits." Then add one gallon of prune juice, peach juice or a sweet wine; one quart of glycerin; one quart of New England rum; and a teaspoon and a half of beading oil.

or different distilleries. They don't place the word *rectifier* on the label, though, because nobody would buy their products.

On the other hand, a large chunk of consumers would probably purchase sexually suggestive labels that pay homage to another set of whiskey salesmen, or rather saleswomen—prostitutes. US brothels were major whiskey retailers in the 1800s. In my book *Whiskey Women: The Untold Story of How Women Saved Bourbon, Scotch, and Irish Whiskey*, I argue that prostitutes were as important as fur traders in introducing whiskey to new markets. In an 1857 physician-led survey in New York City, brothels reported selling $2.08 million in wine and liquor and $3.1 million in sex. This brothel tie to whiskey was so strong that Old Crow bourbon created ads in the 1870s depicting one prostitute dancing while another watched from a seductive chair pose.

This connection to prostitution, however, made bourbon vulnerable to the leaders of the temperance movement, who called whiskey a societal problem. Men left their families for drink and sex. Temperance crusaders used the Old Crow advertisements as a recruitment tool. Around the same time, they also began questioning the medicinal uses of whiskey.

Major medical journals, including the *New England Journal of Medicine*, studied whiskey's efficacy. On treating scarlet fever,

Dr. Samuel George Baker wrote in 1839, "I have been greatly pleased to see the delightful effects of the whiskey ablution. Immediately after it is used, [the patient] falls into a sweet sleep." For treating pneumonia, *The Present Treatment of Disease* instructed in 1891, "If the case passes into the stage of general exhaustion, give whiskey freely."

Despite legitimate medical support, a handful of whiskey makers overstepped their bounds, making unsubstantiated claims. Duffy's Pure Malt Whiskey claimed to cure just about every imaginable disease, including consumption and cancer. Temperance leaders exploited these false claims in their quest to stop the flow of alcohol. In her memoir, the axe-wielding Woman's Christian Temperance Union personality Carrie Nation wrote: "Any physician that will prescribe whiskey or alcohol as a medicine is either a fool or a knave. A fool because he does not understand his business, for even saying that alcohol does arouse the action of the heart, there are medicines that will do that and will not produce the fatal results of alcoholism, which is the worst of all diseases. He is a knave because his practice is a matter of getting a case, and a fee at the same time, like a machine agent who breaks the machine to get the job of mending it. Alcohol destroys the normal condition of all the functions of the body."

By the time Nation published her book in 1908, the government had taken steps to stop false claims. The Bottled-in-Bond Act of 1897 gave consumers confidence that a bottle bearing the "bottled-in-bond" label was safe to drink and not diluted with unwanted contaminants, and the Pure Food and Drug Act of 1906 put an end to snake-oil salesmen's false claims of curing diseases. Meanwhile, the American Medical Association instructed its membership to be more cautious of medicinal whiskey claims and to boycott medical journals carrying Duffy's Pure Malt Whiskey advertisements.

As politicians debated Prohibition in the 1910s, temperance-minded lawmakers could choose from any number of whiskey-related reasons why alcohol should be banned. Going into Prohibition, American whiskey had already had its share of nasty history; it was made by slaves and sold by unsavory traders and prostitutes, it had caused presidential scandals, and it had likely led to thousands of deaths through false advertising and rectifying. Maybe legends are not such a bad idea for selling bourbon, after all.

WHISKEY TAXES

The Whiskey Rebellion from 1791 to 1794 put fear in Congress. They avoided taxing whiskey makers altogether until the country entered another war.

Politicians briefly taxed whiskey during the War of 1812 to pay for debts. From 1814 to 1861 (the beginning of the Civil War), whiskey distillers paid no taxes. However, rum importers paid hefty tariffs, so the government still earned its alcohol tax revenues.

After the Civil War, taxing alcohol became extremely profitable for every level of government and helped build America. It still does.

Today, 60 percent of an average bottle of Kentucky bourbon's price is tax. In the Bluegrass State, schools, roads, and local government official salaries depend upon the lofty taxes bourbon distillers pay.

Kentucky bourbon distillers must pay an aging barrel tax at the local level, a state aging barrel tax of 5 cents per $100 value, a 5 cents per case tax, $1.92 per proof gallon for the state excise tax, $13.50 per proof gallon on the federal excise tax, state wholesale tax of 11 percent, and a 6-percent state sales tax. Until 2014, Kentucky distillers were not allowed to write off the barrel aging tax payments until the whiskey was sold. So, for Elijah Craig twenty-one-year-old bourbon, its parent company, Heaven Hill, paid aging barrel taxes for twenty-one years and could not write off said taxes until the product was actually bottled.[13]

GOVERNMENT AND BUSINESS INTERFERENCE

When Prohibition was ratified January 16, 1919, the bourbon industry was decimated, but it survived thanks to the medicinal market. Nearly a decade before the discovery of penicillin, doctors still prescribed whiskey despite the so-called disease of "whiskey liver" and the medical community's overall mood change toward whiskey prescriptions. Nonetheless, people were sick a lot during

Prohibition and doctors happily prescribed whiskey . . . for medicinal usage only, of course.

Six companies received medicinal licenses to sell 100-proof bonded spirits: the American Medicinal Spirits Company (later named National Distillers), James Thompson and Brother (renamed Glenmore Distillery), Brown-Forman Distillery, Frankfort Distilleries, A. Ph. Stitzel Distillery, and Schenley Distillers Corporation (part of which is now Buffalo Trace). These six medicinal license holders went through their whiskey stocks rather quickly. In 1928, in what's known as the "Distillers Holiday," the government allowed one hundred days of distilling to create more than three million gallons of medicinal whiskey. Distilling permits were also granted in 1930, 1931, 1932, and 1933.

When Congress ratified the Twenty-First Amendment on December 5, 1933, bourbon distillers were back in business. Companies made large investments, knowing the country wanted a stiff drink of fine bourbon. Family businesses were staking their life's work and heritage to the late 1930s Bourbon Boom.

Among these were the Blairs, an important Kentucky whiskey family. In 1876, Thomas C. Blair founded the Blair Distilling Company, built in the limestone hills of Chicago, Kentucky, near the Louisville and Nashville Railroad line. The Blairs were highly reputable straight bourbon whiskey distillers, producing about 1,200 barrels a year. After Prohibition, Thomas' son, Nicholas O. Blair, pushed all the family money to the middle of the table and went all in. He learned how to distill from his father and designed a large copper still; then he built two unique gable warehouses that optimized airflow. Blair said his warehouses made ideal bonded whiskey. He made Thixton-Millett, Old Boone, Thixton's Club Special, Thixton's V.O., and Mel Millett. In addition to making his own bourbons, Blair contract-distilled the Old Saxon bourbon for D. Sachs & Sons of Louisville.

In the late 1930s, small to midsize distilleries like Blair's were popping up all over Kentucky. There was a Churchill Downs Distillery at Smith's Switch near Boston, Hoffman Distillery and Old Joe Distillery in Lawrenceburg, the General Distillers Corporation in Louisville, and Cummins Distilleries in Athertonville. Large distilleries had offices all over the country, while the smaller ones looked to bolster capacity.

Because Kentucky bourbon meant jobs, everything about the industry was newsworthy. The *Kentucky Standard*, February 17, 1938, wrote, "The first whiskey made in Nelson County since the repeal of Prohibition, will be bottled in bond by the Bardstown Distillery about March 1. . . . The whiskey will reach its four-year-age Monday, February 21."

Then, Germany invaded Poland in 1939, and bourbon producers once again found themselves at the mercy of US lawmakers. This time,

WAREHOUSING AND BOTTLING BASIC PERMIT

Blair Distilling Company, Chicago, Marion County, Kentucky
Dated: November 23, 1935

Pursuant to the application dated October 25, 1935, you are hereby authorized and permitted to engage . . . in the business of warehousing and bottling distilled spirits, and, while so engaged, to sell, offer and deliver for sale, contract to sell and ship, in interstate and foreign commerce, at said address(es) and at branch offices and other places of business, the distilled spirits so warehoused and bottled.

This permit is conditioned upon compliance by you with sections 5 and 6 of the Federal Alcohol Administration Act and all other provisions thereof; the Twenty-first Amendment and laws relating to the enforcement thereof; all laws of the United States relating to distilled spirits, wine, and malt beverages, including taxes with respect thereto; all applicable regulations made pursuant to law which are now, or may hereafter be, in force; and the laws of all States in which you engage in business. . . .

Signed, Administrator,
Federal Alcohol Administration

The Blair Distilling Company was a victim of World War II. Grain sanctions kept the Blairs from receiving corn for whiskey, and they went out of business. Old Boone was one of its labels. Like many distilleries, Blair had high hopes coming out of Prohibition.

instead of an outright booze ban, the government sought the assistance of distillers. President Franklin D. Roosevelt formed a whiskey council made up of industry executives to help the government create a distillery plan for the war effort. The Kentucky bourbon distilleries made industrialized alcohol at roughly 190 proof. Since bourbon stills could not reach this high a proof, the stills had to be modified. Distillers added collar columns, applied greater pressure, and reached higher temperatures during distillation. The alcohol never touched oak and would have been shipped immediately to a facility for eventual use in creating grenades, jeeps, parachutes, and other essential war materials.

The distillery community frequently requested distilling holidays, but the government steadfastly denied such requests, wanting instead to stockpile industrial alcohol and reserve grain usage for the war effort. According to a September 1943 Associated Press wire report: "The question of permitting resumption of whiskey output long has been a 'hot potato,' with no official anxious to risk the criticism, which might result from the diversion of grain into whiskey-making at a time of a possible food shortage."[14]

The whiskey brands with corporate backing survived World War II, but many family-owned businesses closed their doors, and many others barely stumbled out of the 1940s. The Blair Distilling Company was one of the casualties. Schenley purchased many smaller distilleries for their equipment and whiskey stocks. The 1950s and 1960s would be a time of corporate growth, making stellar whiskey, and buying up the small producers.

The big names of the era were the Seagram Company, Glencoe, Brown-Forman, Glenmore, Schenley, and National Distillers—conglomerates that were publicly traded or had interests outside of bourbon. These six would buy and sell brands for the next forty years, yet only Brown-Forman still exists as a company. The other five companies sealed their fates with bad business decisions, some of which circled around investing too much in bourbon when it was going out of fashion.

For example, in 1961, the Barton Distillery in Bardstown, Kentucky, expanded its plant at a cost of $750,000 and added state-of-the-art filtration systems, fire protection equipment, and new warehouses, giving the distillery a total of twenty-eight aging warehouses. This made it the largest distillery at the time. They picked up a $12 million loan, registered with the Securities and Exchange Commission (SEC) to become publicly traded with 360,000 common stock shares and filled more than 1 million barrels following Prohibition. But the younger crowd didn't drink bourbon—that's what their parents drank. They wanted vodka.

Five years after Barton's significant risk, its bourbons, especially Barton Reserve and Kentucky Gentleman, were hemorrhaging money. According to the company's 1966 corporate report, Kentucky Gentleman was down fifty-four thousand case sales after spending $124,000 in advertising on the brand. A diverse portfolio kept Barton in the black, but the sagging bourbon economy led to less enthusiasm toward production and deteriorated outside investment interests.

I consider this twenty-year stretch a dark time in bourbon history. We saw the closure of the Old Taylor Distillery and the selling of Stitzel-Weller Distillery to Norton-Simon in 1972. The conglomerate companies executed strategies that still leave spirits business execs scratching their heads, such as Seagram's taking Four Roses bourbon off American shelves and only making it available in foreign markets.

Fortunately, the bourbon makers of the time were producing some of the best whiskey ever made. Today, 1950s- to 1970s-era bourbons are highly coveted by collectors. (In the next chapter, I explain why this era's whiskey is different from today's.) There were a few bright spots during the down times, as well: Maker's Mark, a relatively new brand, established itself as the first ultrapremium bourbon, while Jim Beam created a cult following with its decanter series. In 1984, George T. Stagg Distillery's master distiller, Elmer T. Lee, launched the first single barrel commercially available to consumers. Called "Blanton's," after Lee's former boss, the bourbon changed the industry and was followed by others. Four years later, Jim Beam's Booker Noe popularized the small-batch method, in which he mingled honey barrels together and created bourbon perfection.

The 1990s was a single-barrel and small-batch race for companies that had strong bourbon intentions, while some Scotch- and clear spirits–leaning companies downsized their bourbon operations. Brown-Forman opened the Woodford Reserve Distillery in 1996, while United Distillers, which acquired Norton-Simon (now Diageo), closed Stitzel-Weller in 1992. If United Distiller executives had known that the Stitzel-Weller stills churned out whiskey used in the legendary Pappy

When Woodford Reserve launched in 1996, the distillery, once home to James C. Crow and Oscar Pepper, gave bourbon a much-needed tourism spark. The distillery became a picturesque vacation spot for tourists from around the world.

Van Winkle line, I wonder whether they'd have stopped making whiskey there. The Kentucky Bourbon Festival, Kentucky Bourbon Trail, *Whisky Advocate*, *Whisky* magazine, bourbon blogs, bourbon forums, and hundreds of bourbon-improving experimentations launched in the 1990s, leading to a new millennium that would become bourbon's greatest fifteen-year stretch in history.

Today, you can find limited-edition bourbons that are as close to perfect as possible, as well as value bourbons under thirty dollars that don't break the bank and are every bit as good—for one or two seconds—as the limited editions. But as a consumer, all this bounty can make it hard to select bourbons for your unique palate.

Unlike wine, for which grape percentages are disclosed and terroir implied through the industry's Area of Control designations, bourbon uses its label space for backstories and falsehoods. Although I concur that bourbon legends grew out of necessity, these traditional marketing methods put consumers at a disadvantage for selecting bourbons they like. As Ed Foote, the former master distiller of Stitzel-Weller, once told me, "Whiskey distillers are full of shit." Foote especially takes issue with backstories related to yeast: "You mean to tell me that somebody's grandpappy carried the family yeast recipe from Cromwell to America?" Foote's career started in the early 1960s and ended in the late 1990s, and he's heard a lot of stories about yeast. Take a look at this 1957 Old Charter bourbon advertisement:

> How do you maintain the integrity of a bourbon's flavor . . . keep it unvarying through the years. The man behind Old Charter's answer is to hold fast to the traditions of making fine bourbon. The yeast he uses, for example, is a pedigree strain. It was developed away back in 1898. Every batch of Old Charter is made with cells from this master strain. And every bottle bears its imprint—a uniquely mellow bourbon flavor. He's gone to a lot of trouble to coddle this strain of yeast for 59 years. He went to even more trouble to preserve it in Canada for 14 prohibition years. But the man behind Old Charter tolerates no short cuts. No short cuts in the aging, either. This bourbon isn't hurriedly dripped through charcoal beds. Nor is it double-timed through a barrel. It is charcoal-mellowed the slow way—or seven long years in charred barrels of oak. And so it goes through every step in making Old Charter. It is by any test a costly way to make bourbon. But then, what is the price of perfection? When you drink Old Charter, you mark yourself as a man who appreciates the finest Kentucky has to offer in bourbon. When you serve it to your guests, you offer them a compliment on the esteem in which you hold them.

However, prior to 1920, no dry yeast of suitable stability and with a fermentation rate comparable to that of fresh yeast "had been established."[15] The commercial development of active dry yeast did not occur until World War II, and industrial refrigeration likely was not applied to yeast in Old Charter's 1898 development. Distillers would keep their wet yeast in cool places, but it's impossible to know if the yeast remained pure and without mutation. So the original Old Charter's yeast story that was sold to consumers in 1957 was a long stretch. While this company certainly handled its yeast with absolute care, it's doubtful they maintained the exact same yeast from the 1800s.

Much like Old Charter's yeast story, non-distillery-owning bottlers have been playing it loose with the truth since bottling bourbon became mainstream. Another example is Chapin & Gore bourbon, which was owned by McKesson & Robbins. The company purchased bulk whiskey from the Fairfield Distillery in Bardstown, Kentucky. Like many NDPs today, McKesson & Robbins, which sold the brand to Schenley distillers in the 1940s, offered a lot of BS on its labels and in its advertising:

> In the west of the 1850s, Jim Gore's adventurous life early taught him the importance of being careful in any undertaking. His horse, his gun, his friends—all had to be best in the world. Small wonder, then, that the famous Kentucky bourbon he originated in later years was called "Old Jim Gore—Best in the World." Old Jim Gore Bourbon Whiskey is again available after years of careful preparation to exactly duplicate the three point formula that Old Jim, him self set down: Must be genuine Kentucky Sour Mash; Must be made with "aplenty of costly, small grain—for richer flavor; and must be slowly distilled carefully to make it extra light."

In other advertisements, McKesson & Robbins marketing team later said Jim Gore invented the term *sour mash*.

If McKesson attempted such a claim today, whiskey geeks would tear the company to pieces on Facebook, Twitter, and blogs. Heck, the *New York Times* might even take a stab at it, because it hasn't exactly been a reputable company. In 1938, the SEC determined its books were cooked, missing $20 million of the $87 million of the company's assets. The SEC created new regulations based on the McKesson & Robbins scandal, but from a whiskey perspective, they were no different than any other company.

They stretched Chapin & Gore's truth as much as they could, and they were likely buying whiskey from several distilleries. In fact, selling bulk whiskey has always been a profitable venture for bourbon distillers. In 1966, the Barton Distillery sold $2.45 million in bulk whiskey to undisclosed companies, earning a $653,740 profit. These could have been other distillers needing additional whiskey to meet demand or bottlers selling a phony backstory, but offering whiskey stocks to competitors and bottlers is a storied business practice in American whiskey. It still happens today and is how many companies made it through lean times.

The interesting difference between the NDPs of yesterday and today is that the contemporary companies hold back on marketing the grains and distilling methods. In fact, many modern bourbon producers avoid marketing on these and their aging techniques, while many distilleries refuse to share mashbills.

Just take a look at all the bourbons on shelves today. You see stories on the back labels and clever marketing words like *smoothest*, *best*, and *award-winning*. What you don't see are mashbills, char levels, grain origins, true water sources, distillation techniques, entry proof into the barrel, or other production information. In recent years, there's been a small whiskey geek movement to out distillers' recipes and demand transparency. But just as bourbon folklore was born, bourbon secrecy stems from protective measures to thwart lawsuits and copycats. When Diageo launched the fourth release of its Orphan Barrel Project, it disclosed that the whiskey originated from the George T. Stagg Distillery in the early 1990s. Sazerac, the trademark holders of Stagg and owners of the actual distillery, questioned this use of the Stagg name, saying, "Diageo is attempting to trade on our reputation." After this shot across the bow, hardcore bourbon consumers knew the cold truth: genuine transparency may never happen in their beloved spirit category. If NDP Johnny Distiller buys five hundred barrels of bourbon at Distillery X, which doesn't want this fact known, why would Johnny risk litigation to disclose where their whiskey came from?

Bourbon's only true chance with transparency lies with the big distillers—1792 Barton, Brown-Forman (Old Forester and Woodford Reserve), Buffalo Trace, Four Roses, Heaven Hill, Jim Beam, Maker's

By today's standards, the popular bourbon Chapin & Gore would be considered a non-distiller producer, meaning one that buys and bottles whiskey somebody else has made. Back in the 1950s, however, consumers didn't seem to care where the whiskey was produced. What changed? Visitor centers and the Internet didn't exist then.

AMERICA'S SPIRIT?

By now, you probably realize that bourbon offers a lot of spirited debate. There's no better debate than the use of "America's spirit" when referring to bourbon. This term stems from the May 4, 1964, Congressional Declaration making bourbon a "distinctive product of the U.S."

Author Chuck Cowdery argues since Congress didn't call bourbon "America's spirit," that it should not be called such. Perhaps this is true, but Congress essentially made bourbon the de facto America's spirit. If only Congress had made this more clear!

Hey, decide for yourself; here's the verbatim text. (Is bourbon America's spirit?)

BOURBON WHISKEY DESIGNATED AS DISTINCTIVE PRODUCT OF U.S.

Whereas it has been the commercial policy of the United States to recognize marks of origin applicable to alcoholic beverages imported into the United States; and Whereas such commercial policy has been implemented by the promulgation of appropriate regulations which, among other things, establish standards of identity for such imported alcoholic beverages; and Whereas among the standards of identity which have been established are those for "Scotch whisky" as a distinctive product of Scotland, manufactured in Scotland in compliance with the laws of Great Britain regulating the manufacture of Scotch whisky for consumption in Great Britain and for "Canadian whisky" as a distinctive product of Canada manufactured in Canada in compliance with the laws of the Dominion of Canada regulating the manufacture of whisky for consumption in Canada and for "cognac" as grape brandy distilled in the Cognac region of France, which is entitled to be so designated by the laws and regulations of the French Government; and Whereas "Bourbon whiskey" is a distinctive) product of the United States and is unlike other types of alcoholic beverages, whether foreign or domestic; and Whereas to be entitled to the designation "Bourbon whiskey" the product must conform to the highest standards and must be manufactured in accordance with the laws and regulations of the United States which prescribe a standard of identity for "Bourbon whiskey"; and Whereas Bourbon whiskey has achieved recognition and acceptance throughout the world as a distinctive product of the United States: Now, therefore, be it Resolved by the Senate (he House of Representatives concurring) That it is the sense of Congress that the recognition of Bourbon whiskey as a distinctive product of the United States be brought to the attention of the appropriate agencies of the United States Government toward the end that such agencies will take appropriate action to prohibit the importation into the United States of whisky designated as "Bourbon whiskey."

Mark and Wild Turkey. They make the bulk of this country's bourbon and choose to hide or share ingredient information.

There are a few brands that are transparent about their whiskey's origins. For the most part, though, bourbon brands are selling the name on the bottle first and what's inside second. Bourbon's brand names are the tapestry of legends, truth, and contemporary characters that enticed me to become a bourbon writer. Yes, I love every taste profile of bourbon, but I fell in love with the folksy stories and the real histories on the labels. The true brand stories are as interesting as the myths.

It's time to break out of the bourbon history and regulation mold and get to what's really important—what's inside the bottle. After all, if bourbon didn't win over palates, nobody would care about the history.

PART TWO
SOURCES
OF FLAVOR

PRE-
FERMENTATION

Bourbon begins here, in a cornfield in southern Indiana. Just off a state highway and with black crows circling overhead, longtime corn producer and grain elevator owner-operator John Kolkmeier bends a cornstalk, pulls the

Bourbon must be made with at least 51 percent corn. Kentucky distillers buy corn from farmers in Indiana and Kentucky in a fertile strip of land some call the Whiskey Corn Belt.

leaves off an ear, and shows the insects running around at the tip. "This here isn't GMO, see," he says. "The insects know the corn that isn't GMO and will eat this stuff alive within a couple weeks. We need to probably harvest this pretty soon."

The corn used for bourbon is different than the corn on the cob purchased in a store. When you're buying corn on the cob at the grocery store, you're buying sweet corn, which is plump and juicy and perfect for sinking your teeth into. For bourbon, farmers raise field corn, a variety of maize also referred to as "dent corn." Field corn is also used for livestock feed, industrial products, and processed foods, such as chips, flour, and high-fructose corn syrup. Unlike sweet corn, you cannot pick field corn straight from the farm and take a bite—well, you can, but you're likely to lose a tooth. Field corn is hard as a rock, and the kernels are naturally drier than sweet corn.

Today, the typical bourbon corn is a hybrid yellow field corn that's A1 or A2 food grade, meaning it's good enough for a sack of tortilla chips or a five-star chef's cornbread muffins. Invented in the 1930s, hybrid corn came from cross-pollination and is considered one of the great agricultural advancements of the twentieth century. The hybrid corn could survive during droughts and endure insect attacks.

Since the original hybrid corn strains were developed, seed companies have built conglomerates improving corn's ability to endure weather, insecticides, and pesticides and allowing the seed to grow anywhere. In 1980, the first genetically modified organism (GMO) patent was filed, and sixteen years later Monsanto launched a GMO strain of corn called Roundup Ready corn, essentially creating corn that can withstand heavy chemicals to keep pests down and paving the way for GMO corn to dominate the fields. Planting this corn allowed for larger yields and greater returns for corn farmers, but at the cost of foreign exports and significant public outcry. Both China and the European Union ban GMOs, while anti-Monsanto groups have protested in Washington, DC, and led boycotts against the company. Nevertheless, GMO corn strains have overtaken non-GMO cornfields, and farmers frequently cite higher profit yields.

That brings me back to the ear of corn Kolkmeier pulled from his field. It's riddled with insects and will soon be too damaged to save. He tells me the non-GMO corn fields are a smorgasbord

It's becoming more difficult for American corn farmers to grow non–genetically modified corn. Farmers say GMO is cheaper to produce and in higher demand. Bourbon distillers have been among the non-GMO corn farmers' strongest supporters.

for insects and weeds, requiring more management and money to bring to harvest. Despite the public interest, and increased farmer efforts, and the fact that the non-GMO corn can still grow with proper crop rotations, Kolkmeier says the actual purchaser doesn't want to spend the extra money for non-GMO corn. So, with the passing of the so-called Monsanto Protection Act, essentially ensuring GMO corn is here to stay, corn producers quietly plant GMO corn. This puts bourbon in the crosshairs of the non-GMO activists. Some distillers, including Four Roses, Buffalo Trace, and Wild Turkey, continue to disclose that they're using non-GMO grains. "European and Asian markets won't buy whiskey made with GMO corn," Four Roses master distiller Jim Rutledge told *Grist* magazine in 2012. "But due to cross-pollination, even farmers not using non GMO corn will end up with it eventually. I don't know how many years we can continue like this."

Feeling the outside pressure from media and concerned citizens, Brown-Forman released a statement regarding the use of GMO corn in its whiskeys, perfectly explaining the situation:

> Our philosophy regarding the use of GM products in the crafting of the distillate takes into consideration both the science of distilling and the perceptions and concerns of our consumers. From a scientific point of view, we have never been concerned by the use of GM grains in making bourbon and whiskey because none of the GM materials make it through the distilling process to the final product. However, in the year 2000, a number of our consumers, particularly those in Europe, expressed a preference for non-GM ingredients, and after considering those perceptions, we opted for only 100% non–genetically modified corn, the predominant grain for making of whiskey at our Jack Daniel, Woodford Reserve, Canadian Mist, and Brown-Forman distilleries. Again, we took this action to accommodate our consumers' perceptions even though we knew all genetic material is removed in distillation. Today, we find ourselves facing new realities that require continued study and thought regarding the use of GM grains. Since 2000, the North American grain market has changed significantly. A rapidly shrinking supply of non-GM corn in North America is making it increasingly more difficult to source the quantity of high quality corn required for our bourbons and whiskeys. For example, in 2000, about 25% of all corn grown in the United States and 46% of all corn grown in Canada was genetically modified, while today, more than 90% of all the corn grown in the U.S. and

Canada is genetically modified. This trend is projected to continue and, in addition to reduced plantings of non-GM corn, we estimate that cross contamination will further reduce the amount of certified non-GM corn available.

As the dominoes continue to fall for GMO corn demands, making it more difficult to procure non-GMO corn, it's important to note that the distillers have often been the loudest business opposition for GMO because it impacts exports, while the larger food manufacturers have remained silent. Coincidently, bourbon distillers fought the rise in hybrid corn, too. Former Stitzel-Weller distiller Edwin Foote told me distillers attempted to buy non-hybrid corn, which overtook the farmers' selectively planted best ears. The hybrids could better withstand fertilizers, weed control, and weather, and they would also survive in higher plant densities. This meant the eventual end to the handpicked farmer's corn. Hybrid corn outbred and outlived the non-developed corn, which became too expensive to produce in comparison. Sound familiar?

Ironically, the GMO corn is supplanting the hybrid corn for the exact same reasons it knocked out handpicked farmer plants. Only this time, the bourbon distillers are not alone in trying to save it. GMO activists consistently boycott GMO-made products.

This subject goes much deeper than bourbon, and I've seen the wackiest theories about GMOs. Various bloggers have theorized they will eventually lead to the zombie apocalypse, while more believable opponents offer statistics about how modified crops lead to fewer monarch butterflies and argue that consumers deserve the right to know if a product is GMO. But since this book is about bourbon, I've conducted several experiments to determine if non-GMO corn yields better whiskey.

I'm fortunate to have tasted hundreds of whiskeys made between 1935 and 1960, and between 1970 and 2000. I've collected as much data as I possibly could about these whiskeys' production methods. In one experiment, I tasted two products that claim to use the same exact recipe, distilling method, and aging technique today as they did in the old days: I tasted 1970s Jim Beam white label against today's, and I tasted Wild Turkey 101 from the 1970s and compared it to today's. The 1970s Jim Beam was GMO free, while today's uses GMO corn; Wild Turkey used GMO-free corn in both products.

In my tasting of Jim Beam, I found the 1970s version to be more complex, trickled with a fruitiness undetectable in the modern Jim Beam white label. It must be the grains, I thought. Then, I tasted the Wild Turkey. Remember, Wild Turkey claims to still use non-GMO grains, so absolutely nothing should have changed from a grain perspective. The 1970s version was layered in baking spices, pumpkin spice, cinnamon, caramel, and loads of vanilla; it was one the most delicious bourbons I've put upon my lips. Then, I tasted the modern version. Production wise, the modern juice was supposed to be just like the product from the late 1970s, and its color was similar to its elder whiskey, but the modern Wild Turkey, while still good, lacked a truly inspirational note. It felt like a completely different style of bourbon. I don't know why the 1970s whiskey was better in this particular experiment and the many others I've conducted. But in all my tastings, even when non-GMO grain is the common denominator, whiskey from the 1970s or earlier simply tastes better. Foote believes that the difference is more likely to be caused by changes in water, arguing that today's water requires more filtration; other old-school distillers have told me that the stills just hummed better back in the old days. Of course, there's also the fact that the wood used for the barrels was different than today's wood; so too, the blenders, quality-control standards, and oxidation contribute to the taste differences between older bourbons and those of today.

I've furthered studied the value of GMO by tasting two-year-old modern bourbons with similar high-rye mashbills—one a small-scale, craft, GMO-free bourbon and the other a conglomerate bourbon with GMO seeping out of the bottle. The craft bourbon still carried heavy corn notes, while the large-scale production had almost no corn notes whatsoever. There are so many variables that could impact a smaller producer's product versus that of the big boys, but if the purpose of the corn is to offer flavor, the craft bourbon may indicate a taste argument in favor of GMO-free corn. From fermentation temperatures to proof off the still, the variables are too vast to determine whether the corn type is the reason for a more corn-forward flavor note in craft bourbons. Generally, bourbon distillers don't want the corn flavors sticking around after two years in the barrel.

But I have seen firsthand that GMO-free corn or local corn makes an impact on the flavor. In fresh distillate made from these grains, I've always picked up more earthiness, a rawness that's just not in the larger-elevator-corn whiskeys. During fermentation, I like to stick my finger in the mash and taste. You can taste corn's natural sweetness here at the various stages of fermentation. It's supersweet in the beginning, almost like a mess of corn grits with a dab of butter and brown sugar, and toward the end the corn is a little more earthy with sugary undertones. I've noticed that GMO-free and local corns offer a complexity that's just not in the large-scale elevator corn. When the corn is GMO-free, it tends to be of a higher grade, too, meaning that the quality of the corn could just be better than the GMO stuff. GMO corn is usually selected for its high yield, disease resistance, and ease of harvest.

However, while my experiments lean toward the GMOs having a slight impact on bourbon flavor, I will say my ongoing efforts are inconclusive. There are just too many variables to make a definitive theory. If I were to make an educated guess, I'd argue anything that is potentially harmful in GMO corn—the stuff that will turn us into zombies in 2050—is most certainly processed out during the distillation. For example, another food-label buzzword, gluten, is distilled completely out of bourbon, even if it contains rye or wheat. At least, that's what the scientists told me when I interviewed them for *Scientific American*: "Distilled spirits, because of the distillation process, should contain no detectable gluten residues or gluten peptide residues," says Dr. Stephen Taylor, the codirector of the University of Nebraska's Food Allergy Research and Resource Program. "Proteins and peptides are not volatile and thus would not distill over."

From a market perspective, in any case, GMO corn is here to stay. Since 1978, Kolkmeier Brothers Feed & Grain in Fairfield, Indiana, has supplied GMO and non-GMO corn, rye, malted barley, wheat, and probably a few other grains to Kentucky bourbon distillers. The market for Kolkmeier to sell non-GMO is growing slimmer by the year, he says. "Most of the whiskey people have done away with the non-GMO. There's a few of them that are still in it, but most of them have done away with it," Kolkmeier told me. "Non-GMO was costing extra, and they didn't want to deal with that extra cost. Some people say the non-GMO doesn't yield as good as the modified corn, but I really don't see

John Kolkmeier owns a grain elevator in Saint Paul, Indiana. He's one of the few small grain elevators that have yet to be purchased by conglomerate publicly traded agriculture companies. He mostly sells grains to Kentucky bourbon distillers.

that much difference, myself, if you rotate the crops. If you grow corn after corn after corn, you're probably going to have to use this modified corn with all the chemicals in it."

That said, GMO corn hurts bourbon's ability to feature its predominant grain's terroir as vineyards do with their beloved grapes. Vineyards market their climate, elevation, trellis systems, soil, and various other unique factors that make a grape's origins paramount to what's inside the bottle. The larger bourbon brands will never have this luxury. The whole purpose of GMO corn is to grow it anywhere and in any condition, making whiskey corn's terroir a lot less sexy.

In fact, most of bourbon's corn comes from the same three conglomerate agriculture companies—Cargill, ConAgra, and Archer Daniels Midland (ADM). Kolkmeier is one of the last small grain elevators surviving amidst the sea of giants with publicly traded names. A throwback to the old school, Kolkmeier doesn't use a computer; he still handwrites all his receipts and keeps a Rolodex between his ears. His grain elevator will get any grain for anybody anytime. "The distilleries always seem to call me when I'm at church," he says. "They ask, 'Can you get us a truckload of corn here by eleven tonight?' I say yes. I always say yes. I'm not in the corn business. I'm in the service business."

Kolkmeier has supplied grain to Jim Beam, Wild Turkey, Heaven Hill, and Four Roses distilleries, sending anywhere from five to twenty semi trucks hauling one thousand bushels of corn each to be distilled into bourbon. In good economies and bad economies, bourbon distilleries frequently pay fifty cents to a dollar more per bushel than most buyers. In addition to his fields, Kolkmeier buys from area farmers and sends roughly 1 million bushels or 56 million pounds of corn a year to distillers.

All Kentucky distillers purchase corn from Kentucky and Indiana, a strip of fertile land I like to call the Whiskey Corn Belt. The soils are primed with nitrogen and the plants lightly touched with pesticides and herbicides. When the leaves turn tan and flop over the ear, the corn is ready for harvest. In Indiana and Kentucky, the corn harvest lasts anywhere from mid-September to Thanksgiving. Technologies cut the corncobs from the earth and separate the kernels from the cob. The kernels are then stored to dry. The farmers either sit on the corn to wait for better markets or sell them to Kolkmeier, who always has a buyer lined up for corn.

Distillers want corn that contains less than 14.5 percent moisture, is not damaged or moldy, and is free of toxins. "The reason they want that corn dry is when they grind it, they want a fine grind, and that way, it's like a flour," Kolkmeier says. "If you were to grind, say, fifteen and a half, sixteen percent [moisture in] corn, it would be gritty, and it would settle out in your distilling tanks. So that's why they want a flour, so it just flows." Distiller's corn is clean. To demonstrate, Kolkmeier picks up a handful of corn from a sample bucket. "Dark corn . . . some moldy grains here, see? Whiskey distillers won't take that, but ethanol plants are not that picky. They'll take it." Of course, ethanol is used for fuel and cleaning supplies. Nobody should be drinking the stuff.

WHAT IS A BUSHEL?

Truckers haul corn from their respective grain elevators to the distilleries, where the grains rain out of the trailers and onto conveyer belts. From here, they travel to storage bins and augers, where they are milled and await being sent to the cookers.

In covering bourbon, I learned early on that the term *bushel* is thrown around about as much as *mashbill*. Most people don't know what it means. I asked the lead tour guide at a distillery what it meant, and he admitted he didn't know. I asked the bourbon brand manager, and he didn't know. It's just a term that everybody uses to measure the amount of grain, the manager said.

Merriam-Webster's Dictionary gives two definitions. One indicates a bushel amounts to 35.2 liters in the United States and 36.4 liters in the United Kingdom. "Bushels," according to the world's most widely used dictionary, means "a large amount of something."

Given that few in the United States use liters unless they're referring to soda bottles, I went to the United States Department of Agriculture, where I learned that a bushel of okra weighs twenty-six pounds, eggplant thirty-three pounds per bushel, and apples forty-eight pounds per bushel. As for the shelled corn—the stuff distillers use—that's fifty-six pounds per bushel.

Now, on the next distillery tour you take, when the guide says they run fifteen thousand bushels per day, you can tell the group that that's 840,000 pounds of shelled corn a day.

The distilleries like to tell tourists they inspect every truckload of corn by hand. Well, that's true, but technology still does the heavy lifting.

I rode with a Kolkmeier truck from its southern Indiana home down picturesque state highways and a construction-clogged I-65 to Louisville's Bernheim Distillery, the workhorse facility for Heaven Hill, where the corn is tested. It's given a moisture test and an aflatoxin test to make sure the grain isn't too wet or still containing pesticides. The tester also looks for defective kernels and smells for mold. If the distiller rejects the load, Kolkmeier simply blends the defective corn in with better corn until he reaches an acceptable load. And if that doesn't work, he feeds it to his cattle. "They don't care what they eat," he says. Rejected loads rarely happen, but they come in droves when they do. The most common reason for rejection is too much moisture, in which case Kolkmeier just puts the corn in a silo to let it dry out a little longer.

The corn load I'm traveling with passes all tests with flying colors, and the hopper-bottom trailer drives up to a steel grate. The driver jumps out and pulls a trailer lever, and out comes the corn. A small yellow mountain builds over the grate and falls down onto a conveyor belt. From the perspective of the driver, who works with all the distilleries, this process separates the bourbon makers from one another far more than the smoothness of their products. Bernheim is a driver favorite, taking only about twenty-five minutes to offload the corn. Buffalo Trace can take about an hour, sometimes three, to unload a truck of corn. All drivers love the new Wild Turkey distillery, which is fully automated and takes only about seven minutes.

At the larger distilleries, freshly unloaded corn travels to the silos or augers, where it sits in a holding pattern for anywhere from an hour to a couple of days until conveyors send them to the cooker. In the smaller facilities, distillers pour fifty-pound sacks of milled corn into the tanks. And because they're small, the so-called craft distillers are typically more selective of the corn they purchase, often buying corn grown within twenty-five miles of the distillery. New York's Tuthilltown Spirits, for example, knows exactly where its corn comes from—Tantillo's Farm, Gardiner, New York. Hudson purchases Wapsie Valley corn and local field corn from Tantillo's, while Western Kentucky's MB Roland Distillery purchases the highest grade of American white corn from a farm ten miles from its

Rye is the most common flavor or secondary grain used in bourbon mashbill recipes. Most distillers buy their rye from North Dakota, South Dakota, Canada, or Europe. It's a cold-climate grain frequently used as a cover crop. This bucket contains milled corn and rye.

distilleries. The larger distilleries can't tell you exactly what farms they buy from, because they're buying from grain elevators, which purchase the grains from hundreds of farmers.

But, in the end, corn matters a lot less than the secondary grains—rye or wheat—which distillers frequently call the flavor grains.

The most common secondary grain, rye, typically comes from Canada, the Dakotas, or Europe. Rye was once a cornerstone crop for the Northeast, but as the premiums for corn increased over time, rye plantings dropped. "The best rye for distillation, flavor-wise, is grown in colder climates," Four Roses master distiller Jim Rutledge told me. This is why Four Roses buys the bulk of its rye from Germany, Finland, and other cold regions in Europe. In the United States, rye is mostly used as a cover crop, but whiskey production has motivated farmers to start planting rye for sale as well.

Distillers are looking for rye that has lower enzyme activity in a measurement called the Falling Number, which is the international method of detecting sprout damage in cereal grains. According to Rutledge, rye boasts a very high ratio of enzymes—much higher than that of other grains—and the higher the enzyme level, the more foaming during the fermentation process. If the enzymes are too high, he says, the foaming during fermentation is almost uncontrollable. "I've seen fermenters filled only half full and foam over when enzymes are too high. So the [rye] selection process is a combination of desired sensory perception, starch content, and enzyme level, and the best rye in the last fifteen to eighteen years has been found in northern European countries," Rutledge says. "Cost per bushel is just the beginning of the process, and in my opinion, cost is not nearly as important as the quality of the grain. We could acquire cheaper rye from other sources, but it would negatively impact the flavor of the distillate we produce and ultimately the bourbon."

As for wheat, the Kentucky distillers purchase nearly all of their soft red winter wheat from Kentucky farmers, who use it as a rotation crop between corn or soybean plantings. It's the state's number-four cash crop, and whiskey distillers who use wheat helped keep these farms in business during down times. Maker's Mark, W. L. Weller, and Old Fitzgerald were using wheat in their recipes in the 1980s and 1990s, when Kentucky farmers started planting fewer wheat acres as corn became more profitable; but these farmers have maintained more than four hundred thousand acres at all times, and that's more than enough to supply the bourbons that rely on wheat. As for the geography, Kentucky soil and climate work fine for wheat, but farmers have long considered wheat a profit-challenged crop. According to the University of Kentucky Agriculture Extension Office, with wheat, "there is seldom room in the margins for any agricultural enterprise to generate positive management returns." It's likely that without wheated bourbon production, Kentucky farmers would not be as motivated to plant wheat.

Malted barley, however, will likely never come from Kentucky in large quantities. Unless distillers add a commercial enzyme, they use malted barley during the fermentation process to help control the simple sugars. From a pure production standpoint, North American barley is mostly grown in Canada, the Midwest, the Northwest, the Northern Plains, and a couple of states in the Northeast. It's a cool-season annual cereal grain and can actually grow in many places, but it tends to be more suited for whiskey when it comes from colder climates.

The malting houses are established in the major barley-growing regions and in beer towns. For example, Wisconsin's Malt Research

Because barley goes through the malting process, much of the barley used in smaller distilleries comes in the form of fifty-pound bags. Cargill is one of many larger companies providing bags of malted barley to distilleries.

Institute was established in 1938; the home of Miller Brewing, Wisconsin now supplies much of the bourbon industry's malted barley. Canada is another significant malted barley region for bourbon makers, but all of bourbon's malt comes from North America.

North American barleys, introduced to the New World in the fifteenth century, have become distant cousins to their European counterparts. The genetics, climate, and breeding practices in North America have created a rich variety of malts here, according to North Dakota State University. North American malt barley was bred for both brewers and distillers, creating two distinct types—two-row and six-row. "It is widely believed that two-row barleys are the best barleys for malting and brewing. In fact, outside North America most of the world's brewing nations exclusively use two-row barley for malt. Six-row barleys, if produced overseas at all, are largely used only for feed," wrote North Dakota professors Paul Schwarz and Richard Horsley in the paper, "A Comparison of North American Two-Row and Six-Row Malting Barley."

Whiskey makers use six-row malted barley, because it has more protein and enzyme content than two-row malt. Most brewers say that two-row produces a fuller malt flavor and six-row yields more grain properties in the beer. Bourbon makers desire higher enzyme content to expedite fermentation and less malty taste—two things brewers don't want. But the grain notes barley imparts in the fermentation are neutralized by the corn, wheat, and rye. "We use high-quality malted barley, but unlike Scotch, it is not used for a primary flavoring component," Rutledge says. "It is used for its high enzyme content and conversion of the starches of corn and small flavoring grains—rye, wheat—to fermentable sugars. Some flavor is imparted, but it is not major and it's relatively consistent among the distilleries."

Malted barley converts grain's starch to high amounts of enzymes, complex carbohydrates, and fermentation-loving sugars. The malters steep the barley for thirty-six to forty-eight hours. The grain germinates for four to five days, and it's dried and kilned at 180 to 190 degrees Fahrenheit for two to four hours.

Each grain offers its own flavor profile. Good corn offers no unwanted odors, such as rotten vegetables, and opens the door for the flavoring grains that really dictate a bourbon's taste profile. But some old-school distillers would argue that the grains don't influence taste nearly as much as the yeasts do.

In order for whiskey to be called bourbon, it must be stored in new charred oak containers. At the Brown-Forman cooperage in Louisville, constant flame is caramelizing the wood sugars in these barrels. The popular char no. 4 level, sometimes called the alligator char, is achieved with about fifty-five seconds of pure flame.

CHAPTER THREE

YEAST, DISTILLATION, AND WOOD

Before the corn, malted barley, rye, and wheat meet in a fermentation tank, they're sent to their respective storage bins or augers that mill the grains into a slightly coarse flour. Corn has its own silo, as does barley, but rye and wheat alternate storage time in a single bin. If a distillery does not use wheat, then the rye enjoys its own bin. The milled grains sit for anywhere from an hour to three days, or until the distillery workers are ready to cook the grain.

What happens next depends on the distillery and its proprietary procedures. Typically, the smaller the facility, the more hands-on the process.

At the MB Roland Distillery in western Kentucky, the small crew pours fifty-pound bags of local white corn into a hammer mill, milling the grain and sending it to the cooker. The corn is mixed with malted barley, wheat, or rye and a sour mash for a mixture that resembles a giant pot of white corn grits. MB Roland founder Paul Tomaszewski told me: "The mixture is held to two hundred degrees Fahrenheit for sixty minutes and then is pumped through a heat exchanger to reach one hundred and forty-eight degrees Fahrenheit, when the remainder of the malted barley is mixed in. Immediately, the heavy starches begin to convert to simple sugars and the mash goes from thick and starchy to light and watery with a sweet taste and aroma. The mash is then brought down to ninety degrees, pumped into a six-hundred-gallon fermentation tank, and remains in a climate-controlled room for the five-to seven-day fermentation period. Following fermentation, the mash is blended together, again by hand with an electric mixer, before being pumped into the still."

In contrast to MB Roland's hand mixer standing over the tank, larger distilleries are automated, and workers dictate stirring with the push of a button. Jim Beam's Claremont facility boasts twenty-one forty-five-thousand-gallon fermenters. You could fit seventy-five MB Roland fermenters inside one Beam tank. This doesn't make one process better than the other; rather, large distilleries tend to look more like factories, and the so-called craft distillers frequently execute most fermentation steps by hand.

On distillery tours, bourbon production may seem like it's just a bunch of valves and pipes. These are the pipes of the Bernheim Distillery in Louisville.

At Bernheim and other fully automated distilleries, a worker sits behind a computer monitor and observes the grain unload from a semitrailer and pushes a button to move all grain through to the cooker. Bernheim starts with pouring corn and a little malted barley into the cooker to induce enzyme activity. Yeast and water are added about the same time.

"While the tub is heating up, we will add corn with a little bit of pre-malt. We will then heat all the way up to two hundred and twelve Fahrenheit and hold for a bit. On the cooldown we will add

At the Buffalo Trace Distillery, fermentation takes place in large tanks with ducts to suck out the carbon dioxide. The yeast converts sugars into ethyl alcohol and carbon dioxide, which are released into the air via bubbles rapidly popping to the surface.

the flavoring grain, rye or wheat, at around one hundred and seventy Fahrenheit, then followed by the malt once the temp is below one hundred and fifty Fahrenheit," says Denny Potter, co–master distiller for Heaven Hill.

It's in this cook and the fermentation where bourbon's flavors begin to develop. When yeast is added, the tub begins producing ethanol, other alcohols, esters, aldehydes, and other compounds collectively known as congeners. These congeners greatly contribute to the taste of bourbon and are influenced by the yeast, grain, grain-to-water ratio, water, cooking temperatures, fermentation conditions and length, and available oxygen.

You could say that yeast is the leading flavor component or the flavor starter, depending on whom you talk to. During the cook, the grain's starch is converted to sugars. The yeast, a live, single-cell organism, feeds on sugars. As a byproduct of its sugar feast, yeast creates ethyl alcohol in the process of alcoholic fermentation.

Yeast is literally everywhere. It lives on us, near us, and in the places where we eat, sleep, drink, drive, and swim. Early Egyptians and other ancient peoples used yeast to make bread as well as to make

MAN VERSUS COMPUTER

Since the famous distiller Dr. James C. Crow introduced thermometers, a saccharometer to measure sugar content, and standardized sanitation procedures in the mid-1800s, distilleries have been adding technology to improve production.

For the century following Crow's innovations, whiskey makers followed his techniques and added a few tricks to the trade. Distillation equipment became more industrialized. Rickety copper-pot stills were replaced by towering column stills, and special warehouses were developed just to store bourbon. Today, computers are linked to every aspect of production.

Before the legendary and Bourbon Hall of Famer Elmer T. Lee died in 2013 at the age of ninety-three, he was asked what one thing he didn't like about the bourbon industry. Lee said computers, adding that he feared distillers were relying too much on machines and not the human senses. Another Hall of Famer, former Old Fitzgerald master distiller Edwin Foote, said something similar. "Human senses can be so acute," Foote told me, adding that a machine cannot replace a good nose.

Lee retired in 1985 and Foote in the late 1990s. Both witnessed the computer takeover, in which automated distilleries focused efforts on computers linking to distillery equipment. But the debate for distillery technology goes back much further.

In 1943, Stitzel-Weller master distiller W. H. "Boss" McGill and Seagram's director of research and control Dr. E. H. Scofield squared off in a heated discussion of the natural human element versus the scientific approach. A tried-and-true purist, McGill would dip his finger in the mash and just knew whether it was ready for distillation. He tasted and spit the distillation and nosed the aged whiskey, tasting and spitting, always knowing when the bourbon was ready for bottling or needed more time. Scofield scoffed at this notion. "How can you obtain uniformity that way?" he questioned. "Your taste is affected by too many things. You might have an upset stomach, a cold, or perhaps have smoked a cigar or eaten an onion."[1]

McGill viewed distilling as an art; Scofield considered it a science. These days, the larger distillers probably skew more toward science, but the artisanship is still very much alive. At the major distilleries, I've seen the artist override the scientist when it comes to limited editions, single-barrels, and premium products. But when it comes to the everyday product, in an effort to achieve consistency, science usually wins.

alcohol. But it was not known to be a living organism until Louis Pasteur identified it as such in the late 1860s. Through a microscope, Pasteur determined yeast was responsible for alcoholic fermentation; since then, yeast has become the most underrated and perhaps the most important aspect of making bourbon. It imparts flavor and can dictate the whiskey's floral or spicy characteristics.

There are two basic types of yeast—baker's yeast and brewer's yeast. Brewer's yeast consists of several types that are propagated from barley malt, fermented grape juice, distilled wine, fermented molasses, and fermented rye malt. Today, specialized laboratories maintain strains for current and prospective whiskey clients that range

Distillers use two types of yeast: a propagated wet yeast (top) and a dry yeast (above). Both types offer virtues over the other style. Dry yeast remains true to the master culture every time, while the propagated wet yeast is less faithful but begins fermentation quicker.

from dry yeasts to propagated yeasts. One of these yeast houses is Ferm Solutions, which is the sister company to the Wilderness Trail Distillery in Danville, Kentucky.

According to Ferm Solutions, both dry and propagated yeasts offer unique advantages. Dry yeast is consistent every time, because it comes from the master culture each time the distiller makes a new batch. This consistency limits mutations, ensuring that even after ten or twenty generations, the dry yeast strain will not change into something else. Activated dry yeast requires much less labor, too, while yeast propagation requires intense concentration and skilled labor. But propping yeast is a labor of love and activates the fermentation process quicker. The yeast type is really a matter of preference. Dry yeast users like Heaven Hill will argue for the consistency of dry yeast, while former Seagram's distilleries MGP and Four Roses will swear the propagated wet yeast yields better whiskey.

But all distilleries value their yeast strains.

Most established brands have been using their particular yeast for decades and have it meticulously stored, both professionally and privately: Jim Beam has had the same yeast since Prohibition and stores strains at several production employees' houses. Jim Beam's great-grandson Fred Noe keeps the yeast in his man cave's corner refrigerator, because one can never be too careful about the family yeast strain.

The yeast helps yield the flavor profile a brand desires, and no brand tells this story better than Four Roses. The whiskey maker's identity is practically intertwined with its yeast. Today, Four Roses uses five proprietary yeasts that are linked to its former parent company, Seagram's, which had a production strategy of using ten unique recipes to make bourbon. Seagram's operated five Kentucky distilleries and achieved this target formula strategy with two grain recipes using the so-called V yeast. As each of the distilleries closed—Old Prentice (now Four Roses), Cynthiana, Fairfield, Athertonville, and Calvert—Seagram's created a new yeast to compensate for losing that distillery's uniqueness in the target formula. By the time Seagram's went out of business, Four Roses used five unique yeasts that absolutely set the whiskey apart: V is light fruit; Q is floral essences; K is spicy, nutmeg, and cinnamon; O is fruity with hints of a milk stout; F generates herbal essences. If you taste five Four Roses products side by side with different yeasts, you can absolutely tell a difference.

In truth, Four Roses is the anomaly of bourbon distillers. Nobody else uses five yeast strains; or at least, nobody admits they do. There are so many flavor factors going on in fermentation that it's difficult for individual brands to truthfully know their yeast's impact on the congener production. "The mashbill affects congener production, because each grain has its own sugar and protein profile, which is converted to its own signature flavors during fermentation. This is pretty elementary and can be equated with how bread tastes when you make it with wheat versus rye," says Dr. Pat Heist, founder of Ferm Solutions and the Wilderness Trail Distillery in Danville, Kentucky. "The ratio of one grain in a mashbill relative to another is one part of the recipe. The other important component is how much water is added to how much grain? For example, at our distillery [Wilderness Trail], our mashbill is sixty-five percent corn, twenty-five percent wheat, and ten percent malted barley. This is added to water to yield a sugar content of about eighteen percent Brix; sugar can also be expressed as [degrees] Balling. Other distilleries may use more or less water resulting in a higher or lower sugar content [as measured in] Brix. The higher the sugar, the higher the resulting ethanol and congener concentration. The more congeners produced, the more likely they will be pronounced in the finished spirit. Many chemical changes also occur during aging, which is obviously a big component, probably the biggest, of taste."

The particle size of the milled grains can influence how quickly the starch breaks down into fermentable sugars, but the hope is that the yeast acts quickly on the sugars to mitigate growth of bacteria. Bacteria contribute to their own set of metabolic byproducts that can influence the flavor of the distillate. According to Heist, some distilleries purposely add bacteria into the mix either by undercooking the barley to allow survival of bacteria or by doing a side fermentation with bacteria and then adding this mix to the mash, much like backset is added in the sour-mash method. "Organic acids are a big contributor of flavor to the distillate and are produced by both yeast and bacteria. Each has their own unique acids, but they also produce some common acids," Heist says. "Much of these organic acids and other congeners are governed by the yeast strain, but also things like temperature of fermentation, pH, osmotic stress, level of dissolved oxygen, availability of nitrogen and other macro- and micronutrients, agitation versus no agitation, whether or not there are contaminating bacteria or wild yeast, length of fermentation, how the material is treated between the end of fermentation and distillation—moving to an open-top beer-well can lead to evaporation of ethanol or infusion with oxygen, for example. Whether the sugars are in the form of maltose or glucose, [which is] enzyme dependent, could also influence byproducts lending to flavor differences."

In other words, there's a lot going on during fermentation. But given the success Four Roses has had with its five yeast strains and marketing its yeast, I suspect other brands will begin championing their yeast a little more. Many of them have a great story to tell. For example, after Bill Samuels Sr. closed his family distillery, he professionally stored his yeast in the Midwest. When he started Maker's Mark, he brought this yeast out and tested it against other yeasts, including the original Stitzel-Weller yeast. The yeast that won this tasting panel is still used today. Which one this was depends on whom you ask, however, and Maker's Mark has never played up this story in its marketing.

One area that distillers do not fall short on marketing is the water. In fact, to read a Kentucky bourbon brochure, you'd think Kentucky water was the essence of life and grows hearty men and women. According to the Kentucky Department of Travel, an official state agency, "While it may not be scientifically proven, it's believed that Kentucky's pure-filtered limestone water provides the state's Thoroughbreds with the competitive edge to reach the winner's circle so frequently." Why let science get in the way of telling a good story?

It's true that Kentucky enjoys underground Paleozoic-age aquifers along with Illinois, Indiana, Ohio, and Tennessee. But Kentucky's access to these limestone-filtered waters—through streams, springs, and rivers—became commercialized earlier thanks in part to the access to springs, streams, and rivers. In Kentucky, the water flows over limestone, filtering out unwanted minerals and iron. This is one of the chief reasons distillers made Kentucky home: the water is perfect for making whiskey. Today, distillers are not pumping water directly from a lake or stream and into the still; they must purify it. Most facilities have purification systems onsite and were originally established at the location

Kentucky is blessed with limestone-filtered water. If the water is pulled from an open source, such as this one, state and federal laws still require industrial filtration. Most distilleries filter the water again onsite.

due to the proximity to good clean water. Distilleries located within city boundaries, such as Louisville's Bernheim or Brown-Forman's 354, are pulling city water for distillation. "We'll run water through carbon filtration before it goes to the mash, so it's already disinfected, cleaned, and even more so than it needs to be. Because of the carbon filtration, we pull out any kind of taste or odor elements that might be in that water," Bernheim's Potter says.

The limestone-filtered, purified water is pumped into the tank around the same time as the corn, malt, and yeast. Distillers add the secondary grain as the tub fills, along with the backset. The backset is a thin, milky liquid from the previous distillation that helps kick-start the fermentation. By adding a backset, also called spent beer or sour mash, the distillers are injecting the previously fermented grain's and yeast's flavors to the current fermentation. Furthermore, this technique reduces the chances for bacterial infections. The backset lowers the pH, counteracting the grains' high sugar and starch content, which raise the

1973 OLD GRAND DAD DONA YEASTING PROCEDURE

In an operations report for the former Old Grand Dad Distillery, this is a word-for-word description of how to prepare yeast for bourbon fermentation. Not much has changed.

1. Sterilize tube for one hour at 15 P.S.I.
2. Draw 15 in. of water and heat to 120 F.
3. Add specified amount of malt while agitating.
4. Continue to agitate, heat to 145 F and hold for one hour.
5. Measure amount of dona mash and record on report.
6. Cool to 128 F, then add three gallons of lactic stock.
7. Stir well, take sample, run balling, record on report.
8. Hold at 128 F for seven hours.
9. After four hours, remove lactic stock.
10. After desired propagation to acid of 2.8 to 3.0, pasteurize by heating to 235 F and hold at this temperature for one hour.
11. Immediately cool to setting temperature and inoculate.
12. Stir well, take balling and record results.
13. Allow yeast to work, holding temperature below 86 F.
14. Continue this until balling is two less than one half the set balling. At this point, cool the dona yeast to 60 F and hold until ready for use.
15. After use, rinse the tub thoroughly, draw 60 inches of water and heat to 212 F. Hold for one-half hour and pump through all lines.

Note: Never use steam after the mash has been inoculated with yeast culture.

pH. Distillers could also lower the pH by using food-grade acids, but the backset is much more economical and traditional for bourbon makers.

At the Bernheim distillery, the backset is achieved after the still turns alcohol into vapor during the distillation process. The remaining mash falls to the bottom of the still, where it's pumped to an area that separates the mash's grain and liquid. "It's a simple screen that we run the material over," Potter says. Some of the liquid will fall through and be collected in our backset tank while the remaining grain-and-water mix flows across the screen and into a separate tank, where it will either get picked up by farmers or be neutralized and sent down the drain." Within hours, the backset is then pumped into the fermenters and or mash tubs. But there are times the backset is not used, and this is a benefit of operating an automated distillery. "It doesn't happen often because we abide by the rules of a sour-mash process. However, there are some rare times where you need to dump the backset because it causes too much risk of bacterial contamination," Potter says.

They ideally want an overall fermenter pH of 5.4 on the scale of 0 to 14 and a backset pH around 3.7. Many distillers choose to keep the fermenter between 4.8 and 5.4 pH. If the overall mash falls below 3.7 pH at Bernheim, it's a red flag. At this level, the mash is getting highly acidic, increasing contamination risk and hurting the yeast, which results in off-putting flavors. In low-pH situations, a backset with a pH hovering around 3.5 would continue to decrease the pH and drastically increase bacterial infection potential. In this case, the worker who quarterbacks every step of the fermentation from a computer simply presses a button that indicates "water mash" instead of "sour mash," and water is added to the fermenter. "We will try to use some backset, just not as much as usual," Potter says. "There are times where it is impossible to use any backset, such as when you start up your distillery after a prolonged shutdown. No backset is available, so you are forced to go water. Some distilleries got a little colorful with their marketing terms in that they will call this a 'sweet mash.' All that means is that they did not use backset; they used water. And typically is not something you do on purpose."

Another Bernheim worker in the so-called Head House pays close attention to the water mash, lowering the temperature to ensure the pH balance is at a steady 5.4. Another reason distillers hold onto the traditional sour-mash technique is the leftover liquid is pumped into the city sewer lines, and it can lead to a costly monthly sewer bill.

Bernheim's controlled temperature fermenters bubble up, releasing carbon dioxide and creating alcohol—or, as one Bernheim worker told me, "it pisses out alcohol and shits out carbon dioxide." On the first day, the yeast is active converting starch to sugar and bubbling like a pot of oatmeal cooking. As the fermentation progresses, the bubbles form more slowly, less vigorously, as there is less gas to escape. On the final day, usually around day five, the mash looks like a smooth soup. If need be, distillers can produce beer in as few as three days or as many as seven; manpower and barrel availability dictate how quickly Bernheim turns grain into fermented liquid or distillers beer. How long the fermentation takes varies by distillery, but some believe a lengthier fermentation yields fruitier bourbon.

Once the beer is ready, though, it is pumped to the still. And like every other aspect of creating bourbon, the distillation imparts its own unique flavors to the whiskey. Distilleries have been known to take the same mash to two different stills, using the exact same temperatures, just to see if the stills produce the same consistent whiskey. And the fact is, no two stills have ever yielded the same distillate. Each has its own nuances that make its end product special.

First, it's important to note that bourbon is usually double distilled. The Irish are known for triple distillation, and vodka makers will distill dozens of times. Tradition has dictated that bourbon distillers only distill twice, ensuring some vegetable oils survive the process. At its Versailles, Kentucky, location, Woodford Reserve triple distills with its pot stills, but the final bottled product also includes a mingling of bourbon from Brown-Forman's Louisville distillery, which uses a traditional continuous column still.

Most of the larger distillers use a towering column still that is frequently referred to as a continuous column still, a prototype that Irishman Aeneas Coffey invented in 1830. The concept of Coffey's design was essentially to use perforated copper plates to remove oils during distillation, which created distillate at higher proofs and was much more efficient than pot stills. Coffey's design redefined alcohol distillation and eventually made its way to America.

The larger bourbon distillers use continuous column stills. This workhouse beer still churns out whiskey for MGP Ingredients in Lawrenceburg, Indiana.

At the Corsair Distillery in Nashville, this pot still makes a lot of whiskey. Those who use pot stills swear by their ability to keep the grain's subtle nuances but admit they are harder to clean than a column still.

How it works: The beer (mash) is fed into the vessel, which boils and separates the ethanol from the grains and water. Each compound boils at different temperatures. One compound, methyl alcohol—methanol—is naturally occurring in some fruits and vegetables. Thus, the fermentation byproduct carries over into the distillation process, where methanol boils at 148 degrees Fahrenheit. If the still does not achieve higher temperatures than this, then methanol, which smells like turpentine, becomes the predominant distilled liquid and, if consumed, it could cause blindness or kill. That's why home distilling is illegal and the government cracks down on people making whiskey in their basements. Fortunately, bourbon distillers are cranking up the heat and getting the still to boil high enough—173.1 degrees Fahrenheit, or 78.37 degrees Celsius—to turn the beer's ethanol into vapor. Once the lower-boiling-point compounds turn into vapor, they are cooled to condense into a liquid known as distillate. With column stills, distillers re-distill the distillate to further remove the methanol. Using pot stills, they'll discard the portions of the batch known as "heads" and "tails"—the beginning and end of the distillation, which contain high concentrations of methanol—before re-distilling the so-called heart of the first run.

Inside the column still are perforated trays, usually fifteen to twenty, that strip the alcohol out of the fermented beer, forming a vapor. This portion of the column still is referred to as the beer still, and it strips solids from the concentrating ethanol. After going through the beer still, the alcohol hits the beer condenser, where heat transfer reduces a thermodynamic fluid from the vapor into a liquid. This liquid, the first distillate, is called low wine; it's a raw 90 to 125 proof and not meant for drinking.

From here, at most continuous-still operations, the low wine is fed into the second distillation vessel, a doubler or a thumper. The difference between the two: the still feeds liquid to a doubler and vapor to a thumper. While the column still could pass for a skyscraper in small Midwestern US towns, the doubler or thumper is typically a sexier-looking and much smaller pot still that removes the impurities and further concentrates the low wine into the so-called high wine.

Vendome Copper & Brass Works makes and refurbishes all the major Kentucky bourbon distilleries' column stills. Vendome's Mike Sherman tells me that the distilleries don't like changing a thing when it comes to their stills, even if it would mean being more efficient. For example, the majority of Kentucky distillers' column widths range from Wild Turkey's sixty-inch diameter to Buffalo Trace's eighty-four inches. Maker's Mark's three stills are by far the smallest of the larger distillers at thirty-six inches wide. When Maker's Mark was expanding, Sherman offered to create a larger still for greater capacity. "We tried to convince Maker's Mark that they could go from a thirty-six-inch to just replace it with a bigger still and get twice the production, but they didn't want to have anything [to do] with that," Sherman says. "They wanted to go back with exactly a second thirty-six-inch system. . . . Normally when somebody calls and says, 'Hey, our beer still is worn out, we need another one,' you don't even have to ask if they're going to change anything, because the answer is always no. They want exactly what they got."

The majority of America's still manufacturing takes place at Vendome Copper & Brass Works in Louisville, Kentucky. Operating since the early 1900s, Vendome employs specialty welders and craftsmen. The skill of copper welding is a rare talent because copper is a soft metal that requires finesse and firmness at the same time.

Where Vendome has found some experimentation is in the micro-distillery arena, also called the craft-distillery industry. The American Distilling Institute gives the label of "craft" to independently owned distilleries with maximum annual sales of fifty-two thousand cases. For this genre, Vendome produces smaller column stills, hybrids that are half column and half pot still, as well as traditional pot stills. "When people come to us, the first things we're trying to find out from them are how much do you want to produce? How many cases or how many proof gallons a year or a day are you trying to produce? What size? Once we get an idea of how much people want to produce, not only in the first year but the second, third year, fourth year, they get kind of a business plan, then we'll size the equipment so they can kind of grow into the equipment," Sherman says. "The majority [of smaller

At a 1792 Barton warehouse, barrels stretch as far as the eye can see. Each distillery has its own method of aging whiskey, and this is an all-natural warehouse, tempered only by the occasional open window.

producers] are using pot stills, but more smaller distilleries want a smaller continuous setup."

Whereas Buffalo Trace's continuous still is eighty-four inches in diameter, the smaller distilleries use column stills that range from twelve to twenty-four inches. No matter the size, column stills offer a level of consistency over pot stills. In many respects, a column is a distiller's autopilot; once the still is set and the distiller knows exactly how he or she wants it to run, the steam flows and the column goes. A pot still needs a more hands-on distiller to keep the distillate flowing.

With pot distillation, the distiller outfits two stills, wash still and spirit still, both heated from underneath by either steam coils or fire. The wash—an industry term for distiller's beer—is poured in the pot and boils. Vapors pass through the still's neck and a water-cooled condenser known as the worm, which looks like a winding copper snake. The worm condenses the vapor to create the low wines, which are distilled again in the spirit still, a smaller pot still that further condenses the low wine into high wine. Whereas the column still's final distillation will reach the distiller's targeted proof level, the pot still set up will typically range within 5 proof points.

No matter the still, the regulation is very clear about the maximum proof levels allowed for bourbon in its final distillation—160 proof. But the truth is most distillers are falling into a sweet spot between 120 and 140 proof. The lower the proof as it comes off the still, the more character and vegetable oils survive the distillation. Vodka comes off the still at 190 proof. The US government defines vodka as "odorless" and "tasteless" because not many flavors or aromas can survive a distillation of 190 proof. In fairness to vodka, though, the Polish, Russian, and Swedish production methods offer more nuance for the final product, and there are indeed good vodkas in liquor stores.

Once it comes off the still, the distillate is cut with water and placed in the barrel. Many old-school distillers will say the majority of whiskey's flavor comes from top-notch distilling, but contemporary research suggests they're wrong. Bourbon is all about the barrel.

AGING

When distillate enters the barrel, it's clear as water. The wood chemically changes the whiskey, altering its color, filtering out unwanted properties, and adding notes of caramel, vanilla, coconut, citrus, fruits, and the most impressive smells and tastes you can possibly imagine. The wood is everything to a whiskey, with some studies indicating it makes up 75 percent of a product's flavor profile. And the type of wood is paramount to a good whiskey.

US regulations indicate oak must be used, but why oak? Early distillers tried other types of wood, but oak proved to be more

ALWAYS COPPER

All good stills are made from copper.

Early still makers used copper because they realized it kept the bad smells to a minimum. As it turns out, science proves the truth in this: copper keeps sulfurs and sulfides out of the distillate.

According to the *Journal of the Institute of Brewing*, which studied copper distillation in Scotch, the active sulfur compound in whiskey is dimethyl trisulphide (DMTS), which carries an aroma of rotten vegetables. "Copper in the spirit still condenser also appeared to play a role in controlling sulfury and meaty aromas, but the mechanism for this effect is, as yet, unclear. These results suggest that removing copper from any of these sections in industrial scale stills is likely to have the most significant impact on new make spirit aroma," concluded the journal in 2011.

Copper is also anticorrosive, able to withstand the beating whiskey-making puts on metal, and a great conductor, transferring heat better than other metals.

While distillers will sometimes use other metals, such as stainless steel, to make stills, the inside material touching the mash and distillate is always copper. Vendome's Mike Sherman says, "Every bourbon distillery has copper somewhere in their systems. Some are completely copper from the beer still to their vapor lines to their condensers to the doubler, all the way through. Some have the stripping section of their stills are stainless and into the top part of their stills are copper with the copper vapor line and copper condensers."

durable and liquid tight and to not inject sulfuric or skunky flavor notes like some woods do. In fact, oak offered lovely flavors and aromas that became a staple in all whiskeys.

After much research, cooperages and foresters have determined that the chemical makeup of oak is perfect for whiskey. According to the Independent Stave Company, the world's largest cooperage, within a couple percentage points, oak is made up of 45 percent cellulose, 25 percent lignin, 22 percent hemicellulose, and 8 percent of oak tannins. They've determined the lignin removes vegetal notes while adding

These logs are earmarked to become future Woodford Reserve barrels. The forester looks for tall, straight trees that are about seventy-five years old and have sections of wood about four to six feet with no knots or defects.

vanilla characteristics; the hemicellulose gives the wood sugars or the caramel aspects to the whiskey. When the wood is charred, vanilla, spice, toast, smoke, coconut, mocha, and vanilla are locked into the wood and ready to be extracted by a distillate.

Oak has several species, and bourbon's regulations do not dictate what type of oak is used. Due to availability and success, American white oak, specifically *Quercus alba*, is the main tree used for making whiskey barrels. However, many distillers are currently using French oak—*Quercus petraea* and *Quercus robur*—in everyday bourbons. French oak has nine times the tannins as American, giving these bourbons a spicier flavor profile. Distillers are also using the likes of Mongolian and Japanese oak in experimental products, but these will never become the norm due to supply and cost. In fact, even American white oak is getting harder to come by. Since 2012, there's been a shortage of barrels, making it more difficult for established distilleries to lay whiskey down in the wood and for start-up distilleries to age fresh distillate.

Increased bourbon demand is contributing to the barrel shortage, but the lack of quality wood is even more to blame. Most oak used for bourbon barrels comes from the Ozarks and Appalachian forest regions. Here, heavy rains can keep logging crews from entering the timber tracts, while freezing winters, heavy winds, and tornadoes ruin a tree's chance to become a bourbon barrel. When selecting oak to be used for bourbon barrels, foresters analyze a tree for defects. Knots, broken limbs, crooked bodies, and out-of-line bark indicate minerals and water were redirected to compensate for the tree's imperfections. If a tree loses a limb in an ice storm, it redirects its energy to compensate for the lost limb.

Coopers need about four to six feet between knots in the wood to make a bourbon barrel, as well as a tree that is clean below the limbs and has a trunk with ten to twelve growth rings per inch. Back in the old days, loggers cut any tree they wanted for barrel-stave logs. This randomness yielded leaky barrels with wood either too soft or hard. Today, science-minded foresters look for oak around sixty to seventy-five years old.

"Older trees are not as photosynthetically active as an average stave tree of sixty years old to seventy-five years old," says John Williams, a forester for the Dunaway Timber Company, one of Brown-Forman's contracted stave mills. "Nutrients in older trees slow down."[2] A defective or older tree's scarred insides produce fewer of the wood sugars needed to give bourbon its rich vanilla and caramel flavor notes.

The ideal logs for bourbon barrels are also desired by high-end furniture manufacturers. But the United States' twenty stave mills, which contract with private landowners to find good barrel timber and convert logs into staves, are willing to pay a premium to make sure a tree is used for a bourbon barrel versus an executive's desk.

Once the stave mill manufactures the log into staves 5.5 inches wide and 37 inches long, either the stave mill or the cooperage stores the staves outside for a process that is called seasoning. I believe this is the single most important factor for creating a barrel that yields spectacular whiskey.

"When we air-season wood, we actually let the wood stand in stacks of the barrel staves," says Brad Boswell, whose Independent Stave Company makes the majority of the US whiskey barrels. "The wood is slowly degrading because of the microbial activity that grows and feeds off the wood. The rainwater, snow, and the natural elements leach out the tannins out of the wood."

In my experience, the longer the staves are seasoned, the more complex the whiskey is. The staves for basic, everyday products such

Once the logs are turned into staves, they sit outside, where they air dry or are "air-seasoned," leaching out unwanted microbial particles. This process varies by brand but typically takes between six months and two years.

as Jack Daniel's and Jim Beam are seasoned for six months before being transformed into barrels, while a more premium product such as Woodford Reserve is air-seasoned for nine months. Staves for some bourbons are air-seasoned for as long as three years.

Once dried, the staves are steamed, hand-assembled into a barrel, and proprietarily toasted and charred. Bourbon brands boast about their charring methods in their television commercials, but the fact is, nobody is really doing anything special in the charring arena. All major brands either use a no. 3 char, which is achieved using about 45 seconds of direct and constant flame, or a no. 4 char, 55 seconds of the same. As a part of its Experimental Collection, the Buffalo Trace Distillery experimented with a no. 7 char, or 210 seconds (3.5 minutes) of pure flame, for its #7 Heavy Char Barrel Bourbon release in 2013. The wood was burnt to a crisp and barely held together to age the whiskey. Master distiller Harlen Wheately said the barrel wouldn't have lasted another 30 seconds.

Within a day of its creation, a normal charred barrel is filled with fresh distillate and the whiskey penetrates the wood, typically 75 percent through the stave. "As the barrel breathes, that leads to esterification of the spirit," says Chris Morris, the master distiller for Woodford Reserve. "When we get a barrel that yields a really fruity whiskey, I know that part of the barrel came from a faster-growing tree with softer wood. A portion of the barrel breathes more, and we get a fruitier barrel. Sometimes, those staves will do more leaking."

Speaking of leaks, as the whiskey ages in the barrel, about 3 to 5 percent a year is lost to evaporation. This lost whiskey percentage is

Leak hunting isn't exactly the sexiest job in the business. Crews walk the warehouses, smelling and looking for leaks; if a barrel leaks, well, that's lost whiskey. Leak hunters use old-fashioned cedar pegs, hammers, and other tools to fix those beloved barrels from leaking the good stuff.

affectionately referred to as the "angel's share." Distilled spirit is thinner than water and will evaporate through the wood. It will also leak out of the barrel; if the wood has a microscopic tear from the chainsaw, a baby worm boring through it, or a woodpecker pounding its beak deep in the wood, the stave can have microscopic holes not detected in the cooperage tests or visible by the naked eye. The whiskey will drip out of the wood slowly. Sometimes the wood sugars contain the leak, forming a sappy, stalactite-like tar that plugs the leak. For the times these natural defenses don't fix the leaks, distillers will occasionally deploy leak hunters, who carry a small eight-ounce hammer with a sharp edge to scrape wood fibers; an arsenal of cedar pegs; and a stainless-steel punch with a round bar stock and pointed tip for maximum precision to crush the cedar deep into the oak stave to stop the leaking. Without these three simple tools—the hammer, steel punch, and cedar pegs—the leaking barrel drains dry.

Once fixed, a leaky barrel intrigues people buying personal barrels for their retail outfit, bar, or personal drinking usage. Former Buffalo Trace leak hunter Anthony Manns noticed during samplings for barrel selections that the "crappier" the barrel is, the better it sells. "A barrel

USED BOURBON BARRELS

After bourbon is dumped from a barrel, distillers sell the used barrels to winemakers, Scotch distillers, tequila makers, brewers, and food manufacturers. One of the largest food companies purchasing the used barrels, Tabasco, ages its products in Kentucky bourbon barrels for at least three years; its Reserve sauce spends eight years in the barrel. Tabasco, which advertises its sauces as kosher, purchases all of its barrels from whiskey makers because bourbon is essentially the only industry still using oak that's deemed kosher.

When the used barrels arrive in the hot Louisiana warehouse, the workers will fill them with water and sweat them. They've been known to keep their own used-barrel blend around—"until they get caught," says Took Osborn, vice president of operations at Tabasco.

that looks like hell is a little sweeter and smoother than a pristine barrel," Manns says. "You won't see a lot of people pass up a beat-up barrel."

Theoretically, more oxygen enters a leaking barrel, and the evaporation rate increases from 3 to 5 percent to upwards of 15 percent if the leak is not contained. But does it really affect the flavor? "Overall the leaking barrels do not leak out enough to change the flavor, although there is a threshold where once enough has leaked out that the volume to surface area changes enough to affect the flavor," Wheatley told me for *Whisky Advocate*. "If half the barrel leaked out, it would alter the flavor as it aged."

I wish there were a way to point you in the direction of some bourbon from a leaky barrel, but there's simply no way of telling when you purchase a bottle in the store. I've tasted hundreds of barrels of bourbon, and the top ones always had a little wear and tear, as Mann pointed out. Of course, tasting straight from the barrel can be shocking to the palate.

The barrel-proof whiskey is upwards of 140 proof and contains flecks of black coal from the charring process. By the time you buy the product in the liquor store, the whiskey has been filtered and water has been added. An argument can be made that proofing and filtration are paramount to a bourbon's flavor.

The most common filtering method is chill filtration, in which the distillers cool the aged bourbon down to about 18 degrees Fahrenheit and use a cellulose paper type to filter out the aldehydes, fats, proteins, and esters that will eventually cloud up (or "flock") a bottle if not taken out. The chill filtration might alter the bourbon's subtle nuances, but distillers receive a great amount of returns if they don't do this. When unknowledgeable bourbon enthusiasts see an unopened bottle cloud up from the fats and oils, they are likely to return and never buy the product again, believing there to be something wrong with it. For that reason, distillers filter bourbon. Occasionally, they will not chill filter a product, but they almost always disclose that fact on the label. Several Four Roses private-barrel selections, Elijah Craig Barrel Strength, and George T. Stagg are examples of non-chill-filtered bourbons, and you can certainly detect a difference in the product.

There are other filtration methods, such as the simple barrel-char removal and particle removal filters. Next to chill filtration, the carbon treatment filtration is the most common technique used in bourbon. When used properly, carbon filters can filter out impurities and not bind to alcohols. Woodford Reserve and Angel's Envy use carbon filters, and both brands are able to effectively filter out the unwanted properties without altering the percentage of ethanol.

Unfortunately, the filtration style is not widely promoted by the brands. It's a real shame, because some whiskeys are genuine products of their filtration systems. Michter's, for example, has a state-of-the-art filtration system that yields a much different whiskey than the distiller from where they purchased their whiskey. Michter's Willie Pratt is able to rid the product of flocking but also keep the primary essence or flavors that cause the flocking. He once filtered a single rye whiskey thirty-two ways, and each sample tasted like its own unique product. Michter's products taste as if they've never been filtered. Yet they don't talk about this unique aspect of their processes on their label.

I've found that whiskey companies tend to shy away from marketing the technology involved with their products, citing instead the romance of Kentucky or of craft distilling, thus sparking the spirited debate for technology's place in whiskey. As far as I'm concerned, if technology makes better and more consistent whiskey, then long live the high-tech filtration systems and automated distilleries.

At a pristine Heaven Hill warehouse, bourbon barrels enjoy a little Bardstown sunlight. Each will lose 3 to 5 percent of its volume a year to evaporation, a portion called the "angel's share."

WAREHOUSES

In Kentucky, there are few smells better than what you can get standing in the front and center of a bourbon warehouse, commonly referred to as a rick warehouse, rackhouse, or rickhouse. The aromas of oak, vanilla, coconut, caramel, and spice fill the air. If the smell of bourbon didn't lead to a DUI charge, distillers would probably turn the warehouse smell into an in-car air freshener.

These beautiful pieces of 1800s architecture are made of thick wood beams and sturdy wood floors that will hold up to nine stories of barrels, stacked three high and more than a dozen deep, but warehouses vary from distillery to distillery. Some, such as Jim Beam's, have aluminum-skinned siding. Others, such as a few at Buffalo Trace and at the MGP Ingredients Distillery, enjoy original brick or stone surfaces. Some distilleries choose to open the windows to maximize airflow; others close them tight and control the temperatures.

These warehouses are part mystery, part science, and they're all living, breathing barrel domiciles that dictate the flavor profile of bourbon. Four Roses uses single-story warehouses because they offer a more consistent product, while Jim Beam and others prefer multi-story warehouses, fully admitting the seventh floor gets much hotter than the first and thus yields a different whiskey than down below. Woodford Reserve strictly controls its temperature, never letting the warehouse get too hot or too cold.

The extreme Kentucky weather pushes the whiskey deeper inside the barrel, which expands during the summer months and tightens in the winter. Occasionally, the pressure is so strong the barrel bung will pop off. And the location of the barrel affects the amount of pressure it endures. There are so-called "honey holes" in the warehouse that get the optimum heat and coolness for whiskey.

At Jim Beam, the legendary master distiller Booker Noe called floors seven through nine the center cut of the warehouse because they age more consistently. Noe theorized the bolder flavors were up top. But up until recently, these theories were passed down from distiller to distiller—today, distillers are actually studying them.

Buffalo Trace launched its Warehouse X experimental lab to study the different types of warehouse aging. The small brick-and-concrete warehouse stores up to 150 barrels, but the four independent chambers allow variables to test the aging methods. The variables include natural light, temperature, airflow, and humidity.

Since this studious attempt by Buffalo Trace began in 2013, the University of Kentucky has begun its own efforts to study barrel aging. Once a mystery, aging bourbon is now a science.

When Kentucky Artisans Distillery opened its facility, it almost immediately ran out of room to store barrels. So what do you do when you need warehousing space in a pinch? You purchase containers to store barrels. "You'd be surprised how well these containers age whiskey," says distiller Tripp Stimson. "Warehouses are expensive!"

DISTILLING SEASONS

Once upon a time, Mother Nature dictated the distilling season, which was typically September through June. Back then, distillers were pulling cooling water from lakes and surface water. Summertime temperatures increased the water's heat, well into the upper 80s Fahrenheit. This water feeds the chill-filtration systems and equipment cooling systems. In order for the August and July water to be used, it needed to be cooled. "With the evolution of chillers and cooling towers, it's just a matter of how much money you're willing to spend to keep them running to do the job," says Denny Potter, master distiller at Heaven Hill Distilleries. "In the summertime, it does cost you a little bit more to run those chillers, because they have to work a little bit harder."

Right now, distillers are willing to spend the additional production money to make whiskey. Due to increased demand, most are running six or seven days a week year-round. Better distillation equipment allows distillers to limit fire risk and minimize the sweat-curdling heat. Some distilleries are even adding an additional shift to run the stills at night. "By going to the third shift, you know, we basically added three hundred and twenty barrels a day to our capacity," Potter says.

The modern standard shutdown time is about two weeks to a month. During this shutdown, the engineers are refitting stills, tinkering with software programs, and giving crews much-needed rest.

But whiskey making in the summertime is simply not as efficient as it is during winter. "There's no question that the best time to make whiskey is during the wintertime, because you're not putting the same load on your equipment." Potter says. "Fermentation's easier to maintain, but really, if you have the right equipment in place, it doesn't make a big difference."

NEW-AGE BOURBONS

Forty years ago, bourbon distillers would lose their jobs if they tried to age bourbon in a used barrel. But today, distillers might lose their job if they're not experimenting with used barrels. Influenced by the barrel finishing programs in Scotland, most major distillers now finish bourbon in used cooperage, usually from Europe, for experiments or limited editions. Jim Beam launched a Distiller's Masterpiece bourbon finished in sherry casks. Parker's Heritage Fifth Edition from Heaven Hill boasted a ten-year-old bourbon finished in used cognac barrels.

Buffalo Trace and Woodford Reserve have also released several barrel-finished products. As a part of the Woodford Reserve annual Master's Collection, Woodford Reserve "Four Wood," the seventh release in the 2012 collection, was finished in a maple wood barrel and former port and sherry casks to give incredibly complex notes not usually found in bourbon. While all of the above are special releases, this new barrel-finish craze has also led to mainstay products: Maker's Mark added toasted French white oak staves to existing barrels to create Maker's 46.

Angel's Envy is perhaps the most noted barrel-finished product. Created by former Woodford Reserve master distiller Lincoln Henderson, who passed away in 2013, and his son, Wes, Angel's Envy is six-year-old bourbon finished in port barrels. Angel's Envy has caught ire from the purists for bearing the label "Kentucky Straight Bourbon Whiskey." How can you call something bourbon if it's put in used cooperage?

On this subject, the young Kyle Henderson, Lincoln's grandson, has an answer. "People see port and assume we're aged in a port barrel. We spend ninety-five percent of the time in a white charred oak barrel. We meet all the specifications for bourbon. The only thing we're doing is a finishing process," Henderson says. "The [federal government] has let us and we're not trying to mislead people. It says very front and center on our bottle what we do. We're not trying to circumvent the rules. We're trying to be unique."

HOW TO TASTE
BOURBON

ourbon is not meant to be intimidating. But there are a few tasting methods you can apply to help you pick up aromas and flavor nuances.

When I'm assessing bourbon for competition or critiquing for a magazine, I analyze the color. The darker it is, the older the whiskey and the higher the proof; with each year in the barrel, the liquid gets a little darker. And the more water added to lower the alcohol by volume or proof, the more diluted it is and the paler in color. I score the whiskey's color based on its vibrancy, richness, and occasional hues discovered in the swirl.

After scoring its color, I'll swirl the bourbon and analyze the legs. In wine, the legs are sometimes referred to as wine tears as they trickle down the glass and are shaped like tears. Legs or tears are the hallmark of the Gibbs–Marangoni effect, in which evaporation causes fluid surface tension. In wine, legs point toward high sugar content, but in bourbon, they show character and complexity, offering a slight look into what oils survived distillation and filtration. Longtime Wild Turkey master distiller Jimmy Russell observes that the longer a bourbon's legs, the more robust its flavors. I've also found the closer together the legs are, the more depth and character there is from aroma to the finish. With that

JUST ADD BOURBON

Bourbon has a way of glistening in the sunlight. Due to the use of a new charred oak barrel every time, bourbon yields incredible colors when held up against the sunset or sunrise. These are popular Glencairn glasses that are made for sipping whiskey.

said, I've enjoyed bourbons with hardly any legs at all, so analyzing the legs is more of an observation than a scoring method.

Once I've studied the bourbon legs, I stick my nose in the glass, open my mouth, and smell. By opening your mouth, you release the tension on your olfactory glands. Let's face it: bourbon can bring some heat to the nose, especially when the spirit is more than 100 proof. With an open mouth, your body has two portals from which to breathe oxygen, and your nose doesn't get one heavy dose of alcohol fumes. This method also lets you really assess the aroma.

When you give your nose a chance, you might find these aromas in one of your pours.

Then, I taste, feeling the spirit against my tongue and marking its particular flavor notes. Did the aromas match the notes on the palate? Or did the alcohol burn itself through the tongue? The alcohol burn is not preferred; you want to enjoy the taste of whiskey, not feel an acidic nightmare upon your lips. If you're not accustomed to drinking spirits neat—meaning without ice or water—I recommend a splash of water or an ice cube so your tongue doesn't burn too badly. Tasting whiskey should be an enjoyable experience, not a painful one. But there's a difference between alcohol burn and spice, a character found in most bourbons that contain rye as a secondary grain.

Bourbon's alcohol burn happens when the spirit penetrates down the middle of the tongue like a nine-volt battery and stings all the way down. With spice, the tongue feels a slight tickle in much the same way a hot pepper would. Once you're accustomed to the spirit's texture on the tongue and understand the difference between burn and spice, you can analyze the subtleties in bourbon.

Allspice	Bananas	Campfire
Almonds	Basil	Caramel
Anise	Bay leaf	Caramel-scented candle
Anise seed	Bell pepper	Caraway
Apple, baked	Black pepper	Cardamom
Apple, juice	Blackberry	Cedar chest
Apple, sliced	Bleach	Celery seed
Apricot	Blueberry	Cherry
Apricot, dried	Brown sugar	Chocolate
Baked pies	Butterscotch	Chocolate caramels

Cigar box	Lavender	Pumpkin pie
Cilantro	Leather	Raisins
Cinnamon	Lemon zest	Raspberry
Citrus, general	Licorice	Rose petals
Citrus, lemon	Lilac	Rosemary
Citrus, lime	Mace	Rye
Citrus, orange	Malt-O-Meal	Rye meal
Clove	Maple syrup	Saffron
Cocoa	Marjoram	Sage
Coconut	Marijuana (yes, really)	Sassafras
Coffee	Mint	Savory
Coriander	Mustard	Sesame
Corn	Nutmeg	Sweaty gym socks
Cornmeal	Oak	Tarragon
Crème brûlée	Oatmeal	Tea
Crushed grapes	Orange	Thyme
Cumin	Orange juice	Toasted nuts
Dill seed	Oregano, Mediterranean	Tobacco
Dill weed	Oregano, Mexican	Toffee
Eucalyptus	Pan-melted caramel	Turmeric
Fennel	Parsley	Turpentine
Fenugreek	Pear	Vanilla
Floral	Pecans	Vanilla beans
Fresh-baked biscuits	Pepper	Vanilla extract
Fresh-baked bread,	Peppermint	Vanilla ice cream
wheat or rye	Petrol	Vanilla icing
Geranium	Pine	Vanilla pudding
Ginger	Pineapple	Varnish
Green pepper	Pink pepper	Walnut
Heated caramel syrup	Plum	Wheat
Herbs	Poppy	Wheat meal
Honey	Praline	White pepper

Bourbon's flavor notes tend to skew toward age and mashbill. Or rather, these are the most common denominators that we as tasters can verify and compare in the tastings. Younger bourbons will have more grain notes, for example; high-rye bourbons, such as Four Roses, will typically pack an easy-to-identify cinnamon note. With

If you really want to take your bourbon nose to the next level, go to your local natural grocery store and buy scents to smell and train your nose.

that said, there is one note you should always find in bourbon if it's at least two years old: caramel. If you cannot taste caramel in a straight bourbon, it's flawed. The charred barrel imparts caramel and vanilla in every bourbon, even the bad ones.

As for the nuances you find in bourbon, this is where it gets fun. What you taste will be completely different than what your friend tastes. In professional whiskey circles, we all tend to pick up the same obvious notes, such as grain, caramel, cinnamon, nutmeg, and vanilla, but our identification of more complex notes varies widely. Legendary bartender Joy Perrine, author of *The Kentucky Bourbon Cocktail Book*, finds bananas in Old Forester. Perrine used to live in the Caribbean, eating tropical fruits straight from the source; her palate and perception of banana are much different than mine. My colleague Mark Gillespie frequently picks up campfire smoke in older bourbons that I just describe as smoky. Why campfire smoke specifically? Well, Mark camped out a lot as a kid and effectively discerns the types of smoke he's smelled. As for me, I grew up in agriculture, raising hogs and horses. I'll detail a grainy note that reminds me of the sweet feed I used to feed my horses, and I'll reference to the Jolly Ranchers I munched on as a kid.

In other words, as tasters, we have no recourse but to trust our instincts. Your taste buds and memory are intertwined, and bourbon will tap into your taste bud memories. If you taste biscuits and gravy, by all means, make a note of it, but challenge yourself to further define the note. Is it biscuits and pork gravy loaded with pepper? Or biscuits and a lighter gravy lacking salt? When you taste something and actually think about it, you'll be amazed how easily the mind creates tasting notes.

Once you've completed this portion of the taste, it's time to assess the finish. The finish is how it feels on the way down. If you don't feel the burn as the whiskey travels down the hatch, this represents a smooth finish. Sometimes, the finish offers subtle finish notes, when the whiskey actually has traveled down the esophagus and your tongue picks up final flavors; often, these are the same notes that are the most prominent to begin with. The longer these finish notes last on the tongue, the better.

MY MEDALING STANDARDS

A portion of this was originally published on FredMinnick.com.

As a judge for the San Francisco World Spirits Competition, I'm proud of the job we do in medaling spirits. I'll be honest: we give out a lot of medals. But if it's a double gold medal, now we're talking about something that's delicious. When I give medals to spirits products, this is how I judge them:

NO MEDAL ....Does not represent the category

BRONZE ....Is categorically correct with no off-putting flavors

SILVER...........................Good

GOLD ....Very good

DOUBLE GOLD ....Excellent

BEST OF CLASS..............Stellar and the flavor profile sets the standard for the respective class (for example, Best Small Batch Bourbon)

BEST OF CATEGORY ....In a class of its own with off-the-charts complexities (for example, Best Bourbon)

BEST OF THE SPIRIT ....A once-in-a-lifetime kind of product (for example, Best Whiskey)

TRICKS TO GETTING USED TO BOURBON

In classes, I usually get one person who tastes the bourbon, makes a face, and says, "Oh, I can't do this." The alcohol is just too much for them. Let's face it—bourbon is at least 80 proof or 40 percent alcohol by volume. If you taste something that's 100 proof, half of the liquid going against your tongue is alcohol, and it's like a damn firecracker going off when you first try it. Just as you need to crawl before walk, you can't just jump into drinking bourbon straight out of the barrel.

1. Start with lower-proof bourbons that let you ease into the taste. My favorite starter bourbon is Basil Hayden's, because it's 80 proof and carries some nuances.

2. Add water and ice. This dilutes the alcohol, obviously, but it also cools the temperature, giving your tongue a different sensation to concentrate on.

3. When you smell, open your mouth, so your olfactory sense isn't overwhelmed with alcohol fumes.

4. When you're not tasting, train for the bourbon heat by trickling a little hot sauce on your tongue. The intention here is to prepare your tongue to handle heat, whether in pepper or alcohol form.

WORKSHEET FOR FINDING YOUR AROMAS AND FLAVORS

Let's take a look at special flavors you might find in bourbon. I've found people remember the smells of great times. These questions may help spark a connection between the best time of your life and a unique tasting note in bourbon. I like to call this bourbon mindfulness.

What are your top ten memories?

1.

2.

3.

4.

5.

6.

7.

8.

9.

10.

Now that you have your top memories selected, think back: what were the aromas? Think foods, perfumes, nature scents . . . you know, the surroundings that offer delightful smells.

Name the most prominent aroma from each of your ten best memories.

1.

2.

3.

4.

5.

6.

7.

8.

9.

10.

We've got the good smells connected to your favorite memories. Now let's look at your favorite aromas, period. Be specific. If you love smelling flowers, what kind? If it's your mom's apple pie, is it sitting in the window, coming out of the oven, or on a hot summer day?

Overall, what are your top ten favorite aromas?

1.

2.

3.

4.

5.

6.

7.

8.

9.

10.

You've established smells completely unique to you. Next, let's look at common aromas in bourbon: caramel, grain, spices, vanilla, fruits, floral, and wood. The purpose of this exercise is to familiarize yourself with these common bourbon aromas and how they present themselves in different forms. You can find most of these items at your grocery store and in nature. Smell the following:

CARAMEL

Caramel-scented
   candle
Crème brûlée
Chocolate caramels
Heated caramel syrup
Pan-melted caramel

VANILLA

Vanilla beans
Vanilla extract
Vanilla ice cream
Vanilla icing
Vanilla pudding

GRAINS

Cornmeal
Malt-O-Meal
Oatmeal
Rye meal
Wheat meal

FRUITS AND FLORAL

Baked apples
Geranium
Lavender
Lemon zest
Orange juice

SPICES

Allspice
Anise seed
Basil
Bay leaf
Black pepper
Caraway
Cardamom
Celery seed
Cilantro
Cinnamon
Clove
Coriander
Cumin
Dill seed
Dill weed
Fennel
Fenugreek
Ginger
Green pepper
Mace
Marjoram
Mustard
Nutmeg
Oregano,
   Mediterranean
Oregano,
   Mexican
Parsley
Pink pepper
Poppy
Rosemary
Saffron
Sage
Sassafras
Savory
Sesame
Tarragon
Thyme
Turmeric
White pepper
Rose

Nobody wants to revisit smelly gym socks and spoiled milk, but tracing stinky smells can help you determine what you don't like, and that is just as important for your bourbon adventure as finding your favorite notes. I have full confidence you'll find ten enjoyable notes to each bad note in every bourbon on the market, but training a discerning palate means discovering the one off-putting note in a sea of good ones.

So, what are your ten least favorite smells?

1.

2.

3.

4.

5.

6.

7.

8.

9.

10.

We have established aromas unique to your experience. Let's analyze your palate. Bourbon notes range from citrus to savory and from sweet to spice. So let's take a look at your memory activation for food triggers.

What are your ten favorite vegetables?

1.

2.

3.

4.

5.

6.

7.

8.

9.

10.

What are your ten favorite noncitrus fruits?

1.

2.

3.

4.

5.

6.

7.

8.

9.

10.

What are your ten favorite citrus fruits?

1.

2.

3.

4.

5.

6.

7.

8.

9.

10.

What are your ten favorite spices?

1.

2.

3.

4.

5.

6.

7.

8.

9.

10.

What are your ten favorite sweets?

1.

2.

3.

4.

5.

6.

7.

8.

9.

10.

After completing the aroma and tasting worksheets and studying the common notes, you potentially have more than 130 aromas and tastes completely unique to your comprehension. But like all things in life, some notes are better than others. Please examine all the aromas and tastes and determine the ten you would like to smell or taste in a bourbon. Remember, this is about your preferred aromas and taste buds.

1.

2.

3.

4.

5.

6.

7.

8.

9.

10.

I have one last tasting tip for you, and it's not one used by all professional tasters: mouthfeel. This is common in wine and helps the taster measure the alcohol and sugar levels in wine. In whiskey, I find the mouthfeel is really a way of assessing the alcohol burn and where the whiskey disseminates in the mouth. Some whiskeys are felt only on the tongue, while others can be felt in every crevice, from the soft spot under the tongue to the roof of the mouth. Understanding a bourbon's mouth-feel allows you to separate the good from the great and the best in class. Unlike wine, with its Court of Master Sommeliers, bourbon does not enjoy a governing tasting group that defines mouthfeel, finishes, or general tasting notes. This lack of sommelier-level organization—much like with all things in bourbon—has led to brands marketing their own tasting notes and mouthfeels. My mouthfeel definitions slightly follow those for wine but are unique to bourbon.

ADHESIVE—Sticky all over the palate. An adhesive mouthfeel seemingly hangs around the cheeks long after you swallow. Not to be confused with a long finish, an adhesive mouthfeel dries the areas it touches.

ASTRINGENT—A bourbon with an astringent mouthfeel has a strong alcohol flavor like mouthwash.

CHEWY—A chewy mouthfeel presents a lot of the wood from the barrel and the tannins that come with it.

CREAMY—The whiskey hits the mouth and feels silky on the tongue, falling down the sides like a spoonful of yogurt. The creamy mouthfeel is usually reserved for the very best bourbons, and you'll feel the flavors develop throughout the palate.

CRISPY—This mouthfeel typically comes with notes of citrus and brings desired taste buds to light on a spring or hot summer day. Bourbons with a crispy mouthfeel are typically light in proof, around 80 proof.

DRY—When a dry mouthfeel hits, you immediately want a glass of water, milk, cola, or something to coat your tongue. Some bourbons just suck the moisture out of your tongue, and there is no consistent reason why.

MOUTH COATING—You can feel this bourbon all over your tongue in a warm and lovely way. Unlike a creamy mouthfeel, which stays on the tongue, mouth-coating mouthfeel will travel from the back of the bottom tongue to the front left cheek—it's a tingly feeling.

ROUGH—This mouthfeel stings, bites, and doesn't let up. When a bourbon has an initial rough mouthfeel, add ice and try again.

SNAP-CRACKLE-POP—The tongue literally feels like the snap, crackle, and pop of gum tingling the tongue. You'll find a snap-crackle-pop sensation in higher-proof bourbons, but you could very well notice the mouthfeel changes once you get accustomed to the proof.

SOFT—The feeling on the mouth is quick, intense, and offers delightful notes. Soft mouthfeels tend to fade and don't stick around for the finish.

Undoubtedly, not every aroma or flavor sensation has been covered in these worksheets, and your mouthfeel assessment will depend on your level of whiskey-tasting experience, but this simple exercise has hopefully linked your nose and palate to your brain to think about what you taste. In Jim Beam Black, perhaps you'll pick up a pork rib slathered in Memphis barbecue sauce here and an almond butter parfait there, while enjoying a crispy mouthfeel and long spicy finish. In Bulleit ten-year-old, maybe you'll find a unique toffee or your grandma's custard with a slightly mouth-coating mouthfeel and an ultralong finish. The point is, the tasting experience is *your* experience, and you now have a self-trained olfactory sense and palate ready to compare your tasting notes to mine. In the following tasting chapters, we take a journey through what's inside the bottle to help you pair your personal tasting notes to the styles of bourbon.

GRAIN-FORWARD
BOURBONS

You take a sip of bourbon and notice it's expressing notes of cornbread, oatmeal, and toasted rye bread with a dab of butter. These are all notes of a grain-forward flavor profile, which tends to originate from younger bourbons.

When the whiskey comes off the still, the grain is prominent. As the whiskey sits in the new charred oak barrel, the wood filters out some of the grain properties, slowly lightening the corn notes. It typically takes about four years for a barrel to completely replace the prominent corn note with a caramel or vanilla. With that said, raw grains are quite appealing, and certain consumers prefer younger, grain-forward bourbons to those that are four years old and older.

In fact, at a wedding where I was leading a tasting, I conducted an experiment with fifty non–bourbon consumers and fifty diehard bourbon fans. My tasting lineup included Hudson Baby Bourbon, Angel's Envy Port Barrel Finished Bourbon, Four Roses Small Batch, and Blanton's. About 75 percent of the non–bourbon consumers heavily preferred the much younger bourbon from New York in Hudson Baby Bourbon, while the traditional bourbon drinkers overwhelmingly selected Four Roses and Blanton's as their favorites.

Bourbons that express grain-forward notes tend to be from smaller distilleries or younger than the traditional Kentucky bourbons. With the exception of Redemption, which is delicious sourced whiskey from MGP Ingredients in Lawrenceburg, Indiana, these products come from craft distilleries. All are between two and four years old. Despite their youth, these bourbons can be quite costly and hard to find.

Intrigued by the notion that novice bourbon drinkers liked a younger product, I put another younger bourbon up against Four Roses Small Batch and Maker's Mark. This time, it was an MB Roland Single Barrel Bourbon from Western Kentucky. In this tasting, I educated five hundred convention goers—the majority of whom knew zero about bourbon—and couldn't really gauge the consumers as I had at the wedding. But I had three stations with bartenders pouring. At the end of the night, MB Roland was the only brand with every bottle emptied.

While my theory requires more testing to reach a full conclusion, I believe grain-forward bourbons strongly appeal to palates not familiar with bourbon. At some point in our lives, we've all sunk our teeth in a grilled corncob or spooned up a steamy cream corn. Caramel and vanilla offer familiarity to drinkers, but the grain-forward bourbon's grainy notes offer a gritty, almost raw character that appeals to some consumers over older products.

Of course, the grains pronounce themselves in different ways in different bourbons. Sometimes it will be corncob, cream corn, cornbread, rye

BOURBON SOUR

1 ounce fresh-squeezed lemon juice
1 tablespoon caster sugar
1 egg white
1½ ounces grain-forward bourbon

Dry-shake the first three ingredients
to create a frothy texture. Add ice
into shaker, add 1.5 ounces of grain-forward bourbon,
and shake vigorously. Strain and pour over ice.

bread, sugary wheat flakes, or perhaps a raw kernel of barley (if you've ever had such a thing). The sweeter the grain note is, the closer the grain note is to becoming a full-blown caramel, vanilla, or nutmeg note.

HUDSON BABY BOURBON
Batch no. 4 / Bottle no. 441 (bottled in 2014)

DISTILLERY: Tuthilltown Spirits, Gardiner, New York

CHIEF DISTILLER: Joel Elder was the former master distiller.

PROOF AND PRODUCT AGE: 92 proof. Hudson Baby Bourbon has no age statement but contains barrels between 1 and 2.5 years old.

MASHBILL: 90 percent corn, 10 percent barley (former productions were 100 percent corn)

GRAIN ORIGINS: The corn comes from Tantillo's Farm and Wapsie Valley Corn as well as the distillery's local field corn. Tuthilltown uses Canadian malted barley.

DISTILLATION: Copper pots with fractioning columns (Christian Carl). Double distilled.

BARREL ENTRY PROOF: 114

AGING: The wood used is mostly Missouri American white oak with a few Pennsylvania American white oaks. Barrels range from 10 to 53 gallons with a no. 3 and no. 4 char. Hudson Baby Bourbon uses bass speakers to allow sound waves to drive whiskey deeper into the wood. Its age can be measured by the barrels used: the 10-gallon barrels average around a year old, while the traditional 53-gallon barrels skew 2.5 years and older. When all barrels are mingled, Baby Bourbon ranges between 20 and 48 months.

BARRELS PER BOTTLING: With Hudson products, the number of barrels per dump is constantly changing because they blend 4 different barrel sizes, ranging from 10 gallons to 53 gallons. However, each bottling contains about 800 gallons of whiskey.

FILTERING METHOD: Cotton micron filtration to remove char from barrels. No chilling or charcoal methods used for the Hudson line.

COLOR: For such a young bourbon that is only 46 percent alcohol by volume, Hudson Baby Bourbon offers an extraordinarily rich color that rivals bourbons three times its age.

NOSE: The aging method certainly appears on the nose with resounding wood fibers appearing on first whiff. After the wood dissipates, a lush, sweet grain follows with just a hint of cardamom, caramel, and vanilla.

PALATE: In addition to notes found in the nose, Hudson has a unique smoke that's almost like the burnt top layer of a crème brûlée; you might find it to be a burnt vanilla or a charred marshmallow. This quality makes the New York bourbon a fun change of pace from Kentucky bourbons. A slightly soft mouthfeel.

FINISH: After the whiskey goes down, a subtle spice gives a lovely finish.

COMPARE THOUGHTS

Did you pick up the grain note?

YOUR TASTING NOTES:

MBR KENTUCKY BOURBON WHISKEY

Batch no. 14 / Bottle no. 73 of 120

DISTILLERY: MB Roland Distillery, Pembroke Kentucky

MASTER DISTILLER: Paul Tomaszewski

PROOF AND PRODUCT AGE: 104.21 proof. No age statement, but the bourbon is around 2 years old.

MASHBILL: 75 percent white corn, 15 percent rye, 10 percent malted barley

M
B
R

PEMBROKE **STILL & BARREL PROOF**
CHRISTIAN CO. KY **STILL & BARREL PROOF**

KEN
BOU
WHI

DISTILLER'S REC

BATCH	
14	
BARREL	

#4 Cha

52 · 105 ALC

Uncut & a

still to the

GRAIN ORIGINS: Bagged local white corn comes from Christian County Grain, which is 5 miles from the distillery. Rye and malted barley originate from the Midwest.

DISTILLATION: The double-distilled whiskey comes off the 600-gallon pot still at 110 proof and goes straight into the barrel.

BARREL ENTRY PROOF: 110

AGING: MB Roland purchases wine-grade barrels from the Independent Stave Company, which procures white oak throughout North America.

BARRELS PER BOTTLING: 1

FILTERING METHOD: Non-chill filtration

COLOR: This whiskey is above 100 proof, but it's around 2 years old. It's lighter in color than Wild Turkey 101, an older bourbon in the same approximate proof range. Nonetheless, it's a solid light brown color, which indicates the whiskey maximized its time in the wood.

NOSE: This is one of the most beautiful bouquets in a young bourbon you'll ever find. Screaming of vanilla cake batter, toasted almonds, praline, caramel, and a hint of citrus, MB Roland brings pure joy to a whiskey lover looking for something different in bourbon.

PALATE: While the nose offers a cake-batter smell, the palate is like dipping your finger in the bowl and just taking a lick. Following caramel, vanilla, leather and tobacco, the bourbon gives a tickle of cinnamon.

FINISH: Soft. I am left wondering what this whiskey will taste like if left in the barrel for another couple of years. It shows so much promise.

COMPARE THOUGHTS

Compare this bourbon's color to that of an older bourbon. Do you find MB Roland is exceptional in color for its age?

YOUR TASTING NOTES:

REDEMPTION HIGH RYE BOURBON
Straight Bourbon Whiskey / Batch no. 14 / Bottle no. 2293

DISTILLERY: MGP Ingredients Distillery, Lawrenceburg, Indiana

MASTER DISTILLER: Greg Metze, who is not affiliated with this brand. Redemption owners purchase whiskey stocks from MGP and bottle the whiskey in Bardstown, Kentucky.

PROOF AND PRODUCT AGE: 92 proof. 2 to 3 years old.

MASHBILL: 60 percent corn, 38.2 percent rye, 1.8 percent malted barley

GRAIN ORIGINS: Indiana for the corn. Rye originates from Europe, while the malted barley is purchased from MaltEurop in Milwaukee, Wisconsin.

DISTILLATION: MGP Ingredients double distills whiskey using a 48- or 72-inch-diameter Vendome column still and one of 2 doublers that are 15,000 and 40,000 gallons in capacity.

BARREL ENTRY PROOF: 120

AGING: These are standard Independent Stave Barrels purchased by MGP Ingredients—American white oak with a char no. 3 or 4.

BARRELS PER BOTTLING: 7 to 10

FILTERING METHOD: Chill filtration

COLOR: Barn straw

NOSE: This younger whiskey with a boatload of rye sure smells of perfume scents. It's also packing hints of spice and a little caramel.

PALATE: A much different sensory experience than the nose, offering a crisp mouthfeel and notes of herbs, burnt corn, and spice.

FINISH: A short, cinnamon finish.

COMPARE THOUGHTS
The grain note expresses itself differently in this bourbon because the grain is burnt, almost spicy. Can you detect a raw grain?

YOUR TASTING NOTES:

FEW BOURBON WHISKEY
Bourbon Whiskey / Small media sample

DISTILLERY: FEW Spirits, Evanston, Illinois

MASTER DISTILLER: Paul Hletko

PROOF AND PRODUCT AGE: 93 proof. No age statement, but the bourbon is under 4 years old.

MASHBILL: High rye with a spicy yeast. The distiller does not disclose its mashbill, and it is not publicly available.

GRAIN ORIGINS: Non-GMO corn and rye grown within 100 miles of the distillery and malted barley purchased from the Briess Malt & Ingredients Company.

DISTILLATION: The low wine is produced with a 12-inch-diameter Vendome column still. The second distillation runs off a 1,500-liter hybrid still.

BARREL ENTRY PROOF: 118

AGING: FEW purchases barrels from 2 cooperages that source American white oak from Missouri and northern states. They use 15-, 30-, and 53-gallon barrels. Barrels are char no. 3.

BARRELS PER BOTTLING: Since there are so many barrel sizes, this is a difficult question to answer, but FEW shoots for target dumps of 75 to 100 gallons and 200 to 300 gallons.

FILTERING METHOD: Pad filter to remove char

COLOR: Dark straw

NOSE: Oh boy, this bouquet has a life of its own. We're talking cornbread fresh out of the oven, vanilla, red pepper flakes, clove, and a hint of cardamom.

PALATE: The cornbread note is subtle here and immediately warms up to woodiness and saddle leather. It's herbal with hints of vanilla and caramel.

FINISH: For such a young bourbon, FEW Spirits has a finish that keeps tickling long after it's down the hatch. I find subtle hints of oak and vanilla on this lovely, long finish.

COMPARE THOUGHTS
In the nose, did you pick up the incredible spice?

YOUR TASTING NOTES:

MCKENZIE
Single Barrel Bourbon Whiskey / Barrel no. 413

DISTILLERY: Finger Lakes Distilling, Burdett, New York

MASTER DISTILLER: Thomas McKenzie

PROOF AND PRODUCT AGE: 102.4 proof. 44 months.

MASHBILL: 70 percent corn, 20 percent white wheat, and 10 percent malted barley

GRAIN ORIGINS: Corn and wheat come from a farm 5 miles from the distillery. Malt is a Canadian distiller's malt.

DISTILLATION: This whiskey is single-pot distilled through the rectifying column and when done is about 115 proof.

BARREL ENTRY PROOF: 100

AGING: Made by McGinnis wood products, the 53-gallon American white oak barrel is air-seasoned for 36 months and given a char no. 4. Aged in barrel racks similar to what you see in wineries. McKenzie cycles heat during the winter.

BARRELS PER BOTTLING: 1

FILTERING METHOD: None

COLOR: Light brown

NOSE: Fresh grain with herbs. This is the kind of nose that makes me want to become a vegetarian—it's ripe with vegetable notes and herbal essence in a good way.

PALATE: The mouthfeel is chewy, and the grains establish themselves as lovely corn on the cob with a pat of butter, salt, and pepper. The herbs remain heavy, yielding oregano and basil notes, but it's a myriad of herbs, and they come quickly.

FINISH: Medium

COMPARE THOUGHTS
Did you pick up the herbal notes?

YOUR TASTING NOTES:

SMOOTH AMBLER YEARLING
Small Batch / Premium Cut / Batch no. 15 / Bottled on July 10, 2014, by Sarah

DISTILLERY: Smooth Ambler, Maxwelton, West Virginia

MASTER DISTILLER: John Flora

PROOF AND PRODUCT AGE: 92 proof. 2 years, 11 months old.

MASHBILL: 73 percent corn, 15 percent wheat, 12 percent malted barley

GRAIN ORIGINS: Wheat and corn are West Virginia, while malt is Cargill distiller's malt.

DISTILLATION: Double distilled on a 12-inch-diameter column and a 50-gallon doubler.

BARREL ENTRY PROOF: Varies from 100 to 120, but the most frequent is 117.2 proof into the barrel.

AGING: 53-gallon barrels include American white oak seasoned for 1 year and then charred with no. 3 and no. 4 chars. Barrels age in concrete warehouses.

BARRELS PER BOTTLING: 1 or 2

FILTERING METHOD: A stainless-steel mesh removes barrel bits. Whiskey is run through a small filter to remove any char and filtered again moments before bottling.

COLOR: Gold bullion with caramel hues

NOSE: This bourbon's nose could easily get lost in flight, because it's bringing forth aromas that are not as bold as older bourbon. I pick up floral notes, fresh milled corn, caramel, vanilla, and just a hint of toasted marshmallow.

PALATE: Brings out a chewy roasted corn note that's quite lovely and reminds me of campfire corn. Caramel, vanilla, and a spicy tea with hints of cinnamon and lavender follow. The mouthfeel is a combination of soft and dry.

FINISH: Short and spicy

COMPARE THOUGHTS
Was this palate smoky and corny all at the same time for you?

YOUR TASTING NOTES:

TOWN BRANCH
Kentucky Straight Bourbon Whiskey

DISTILLERY: Town Branch Distillery, Lexington, Kentucky

MASTER DISTILLER: Mark Coffman

PROOF AND PRODUCT AGE: 80 proof. At least 2 years old.

MASHBILL: 72 percent corn, 15 percent malted rye, and 13 percent malted barley.

GRAIN ORIGINS: Town Branch purchases gelatinized corn, malted barley, and malted rye from Cargill.

DISTILLATION: Forsyth Pot still double distillation with 5,000-liter wash still and 3,200-liter spirit still.

BARREL ENTRY PROOF: 120

AGING: Town Branch uses char no. 5 Independent Stave barrels and contract ages at Kentucky Bourbon Distillers.

FILTERING METHOD: Chill filtering in a pall filtration system.

COLOR: Straw

NOSE: Freshly peeled corn grilling under a charcoal flame. After this, oak and banana fill the nose.

PALATE: Loaded with pear and banana, with caramel and vanilla making a nice rush to the finish over a rough mouthfeel.

FINISH: Short, with cinnamon

COMPARE THOUGHTS
This seemed to have loads of banana. Did you get this?

YOUR TASTING NOTES:

Cyrus Noble has been around a long time. Today, it's been labeled as another sourced whiskey product, but the brand's genuine history offers a unique legacy in American whiskey. In 1901, a man literally traded a gold mine just for a quart of Cyrus Noble whiskey.

CHAPTER SIX

NUTMEG-FORWARD
BOURBONS

Imagine bourbon upon your lips that offers a strikingly similar flavor note to the eggnog you buy every year for the holidays. It's not quite the same as the eggnog; in fact, that might be pumpkin pie or the mystery spice in mom's meatballs you're tasting. This, my friends, is nutmeg, an incredibly common note in bourbons. Unlike the common notes of caramel or vanilla, nutmeg often falls short of making the tasting notes, because the note—while present—is often difficult to describe. This is why it sometimes appears as eggnog, pumpkin pie, or toasted nuts. Regardless, nutmeg shows itself in a multitude of bourbons one way or another; the only common denominator I've found in these nutmeg-forward bourbons is higher barley percentages in the mashbills, but as you will see, this is not a steadfast rule. In many respects, nutmeg remains a mystery note. For sure, much tasting and studying must be done to get to the bottom of this nuance!

Interestingly, you'll find nutmeg in bourbons that also yield cinnamon and cloves. Bakers use all three spices to create delicious baked goods and icings. And just like the spice from the nutmeg tree, nutmeg-forward bourbons tend to be extremely savory.

Nutmeg-forward bourbons tend to come from a family of similar mashbills with equal parts rye and malted barley. They are pleasing, affordable, and relatively easy to find.

ANGEL'S ENVY

Small Batch Bourbon Whiskey

DISTILLERY: Currently, Angel's Envy is distilled at 3 undisclosed locations, but the company is constructing its own distillery that the company hopes is operating by the end of 2015.

MASTER DISTILLER: Unknown. Prior to his passing, Lincoln Henderson served as the de facto master distiller, but he was really more of a master blender, since he was not distilling his own whiskey.

PROOF AND PRODUCT AGE: 86.6 proof. No age statement.

MASHBILL: Angel's Envy originally purchased large quantities of barrels from sourced whiskey suppliers. These original barrels were a hodgepodge of mashbills, and the mashbill content is unknown. Since the brand started contract-distilling its own recipe, the mashbill is 72 percent corn, 18 percent rye, and 10 percent malted barley.

GRAIN ORIGINS: All corn is from Kentucky and Indiana. Rye is from the Dakotas, and malted barley originates from Canada.

DISTILLATION: Column and then doubler.

BARREL ENTRY PROOF: 125. Once the new distiller is up and running, Angel's Envy hopes the barrel entry proof will be 107.

AGING: After its medium rye mashbill is distilled, Angel's Envy barrels are aged at Stitzel-Weller in Louisville, Willett in Bardstown, and Strong Spirits in Bardstown. Since Angel's Envy uses Independent Stave Company for its bourbon barrels, the wood comes from the Ozarks and Appalachian areas with the barrels boasting a no. 3 char. The port barrels are purchased through a broker and are not from one specific winery. After aging in bourbon barrels for 6 years, Angel's Envy is finished in port barrels for 4 to 7 months.

BARRELS PER BOTTLING: 12 to 13 bourbon barrels are poured into 10 port barrels, which are then dumped for bottling after reaching optimal age.

FILTERING METHOD: Carbon filtration

COLOR: Russet

NOSE: Whipped cream, chocolate, caramel, vanilla extract, and spice with a slight hint of campfire smoke.

PALATE: A warm and creamy mouthfeel gently coats the tongue with nose of chocolate brownies, nutmeg, black pepper, raspberry jam, and caramel candies.

FINISH: Short to medium with a spicy kick

COMPARE THOUGHTS
Did you get whipped cream on the nose?

YOUR TASTING NOTES:

JEFFERSON'S OCEAN
Straight Bourbon Whiskey / Very Small Batch / Batch no. 19 / Bottle no. 0181

DISTILLERY: Unknown. Jefferson's purchases barrels on wholesale receipts from several distilleries.

MASTER DISTILLER: Unknown. The master blender is Trey Zoeller.

PROOF AND PRODUCT AGE: 90 proof. No age statement.

MASHBILL: For all of Jefferson's mainstay products, unless noted on the bottle, there are 3 to 4 recipes of ages ranging from 6 to 12 years old. All recipes contain rye, but 1 high-rye recipe constitutes 55 percent of the bottling in Jefferson's bourbons.

GRAIN ORIGINS: Same as most Kentucky distillers—corn from Indiana and Kentucky, rye and barley from the Midwest and Canada.

DISTILLATION: Double

BARREL ENTRY PROOF: 125

AGING: Jefferson's barrels use a char no. 2. For the Jefferson's Ocean, barrels are sent around the world on a 126-foot research vessel. Jefferson's 6-year-old barrels hit 30 ports across the equator over 6 months. They're bottled immediately after the ship ports.

BARRELS PER BOTTLING: Prior to 2014, only a handful of barrels were on the ships. Now, 390 Jefferson's barrels are at sea. It's unknown how many go into a batch.

FILTERING METHOD: Chill filtration

COLOR: Caramel

NOSE: As expected, there's a briny quality to this, but this note fades quickly, giving way to caramel, nutmeg, and vanilla with some spice.

PALATE: Salted caramel, oyster shell, and vanilla custard lead this charge in one of the more unique first-impression palates in all of bourbon. It's extremely spicy with notes of cinnamon and black pepper. Nutmeg surfaces toward the end.

FINISH: Medium with cinnamon

COMPARE THOUGHTS

Compared to the other bourbons you've had thus far, how different was this one?

YOUR TASTING NOTES:

CYRUS NOBLE
Small Batch Bourbon Whiskey

DISTILLERY: The current bottlings originate from the former Charles Medley Distillery in Owensboro and were brokered by the Heaven Hill Distillery. This whiskey was once intended for the Wathen's bourbon line.

MASTER DISTILLER: Charles Medley was the last master distiller at the Charles Medley Distillery, which was named after his ancestor of the same name.

PROOF AND PRODUCT AGE: 90 Proof. No age statement, but the batch includes 5- to 6-year-old bourbon.

MASHBILL: 75 percent corn, 17 percent rye, 8 percent malted barley

GRAIN ORIGINS: Unknown, but most likely Indiana, Kentucky, and Illinois for corn and Canada for the rye and barley

DISTILLATION: Unknown

BARREL ENTRY PROOF: 120

AGING: Aged in the Missouri Ozarks on contract with the Heaven Hill Distillery. No. 3 char is used on the barrels.

BARRELS PER BOTTLING: 15 to 25

FILTERING METHOD: Chill filtration

COLOR: Light brown with vibrant dark caramel hues

NOSE: Toasted caramel, fudge, peanut brittle, fresh-baked cinnamon bread, and vanilla extract.

PALATE: This has a snap-crackle-pop mouthfeel with a lot of peppery spice. Despite having a moderate rye level, Cyrus Noble packs a lot of spice, in all forms of baking spices, allspice, peppers, cinnamon, and nutmeg. But it's the sweetness, in the form of a salted caramel and a praline, that balances this very nice bourbon.

FINISH: Medium and spicy

COMPARE THOUGHTS
Did you pick up the snap-crackle-pop mouthfeel?

YOUR TASTING NOTES:

SELECT HEAVEN HILL DISTILLERY BRANDS: ELIJAH CRAIG, EVAN WILLIAMS LABELS, FIGHTING COCK, AND HENRY MCKENNA

Note: These products share the same mashbill and aging techniques.

DISTILLERY: Heaven Hill's Bernheim Distillery in Louisville

MASTER DISTILLER: Prior to 2013, Parker Beam was the master distiller for these products. His son, Craig, shared in these duties, but Parker has taken a medical leave of absence to battle ALS and Craig has moved into a consultancy role with the same duties as before. In late 2014, Heaven Hill named Denny Potter co–master distiller.

MASHBILL: 78 percent corn, 12 percent malted barley, 10 percent rye

GRAIN ORIGINS: Corn comes from Kentucky and Indiana, while rye comes primarily from the Dakotas and Canada. The barley is typically grown in Minnesota, the Dakotas, and Washington but is malted in Wisconsin.

BOURBON BLUEBERRY SMASH

4 fresh blackberries

1½ ounces fresh sweet-and-sour mix

¼ ounce simple syrup with a dash
    of vanilla extract

½ ounce crème de cassis

1½ ounce nutmeg-forward bourbon

Muddle blackberries with the sweet-and-sour mix, add other ingredients, and shake vigorously. Strain and pour over ice. Garnish with sprig of mint.

This recipe is a take on award-winning mixologist Patricia Richards's Sinatra Smash, which uses Gentleman Jack Tennessee Whiskey (as well as vanilla-infused simple syrup in place of the extract I suggest here). Richards's recipe was created for the Wynn Las Vegas hotels and has become a Las Vegas staple.

DISTILLATION: Distilled at the Bernheim distillery, Heaven Hill brands are created on 2 66-inch-diameter, 70-foot-tall column stills with 1 thumper. All products are double distilled.

BARREL ENTRY PROOF: 125

AGING: Heaven Hill uses several coopers to create its barrels. Independent Stave Company and McGinnis Cooperage are the 2 main coopers, both of which source American white oak wood from the Ozarks and Appalachian areas. All barrels come with a no. 3 char. They rest in Heaven Hill's aluminum-skinned warehouses in Bardstown.

FILTERING METHOD: Chill filtered unless otherwise noted

ELIJAH CRAIG BARREL STRENGTH
Kentucky Straight Bourbon Whiskey

PROOF AND PRODUCT AGE: 133.2 proof. 12 years old.

FILTERING METHOD: Non–chill filtration; instead, a light filtration is used to remove barrel-char flakes

BARRELS PER BOTTLING: 70 to 100

COLOR: Ultra dark amber, nearly a deep brown

NOSE: This is 133.2 proof? I picked up faint senses of alcohol, but that was lost in the voyage of rich caramels, powerful vanillas, toasted cinnamon cereal, and oak.

PALATE: There's little burn compared to other bourbons of similar proof. The mouthfeel is surprisingly coating and creamy, with a party of pies going on in the middle of the tongue: apple, cherry, blueberry, and even pumpkin offer resounding and convincing notes after a soirée of pecans and caramel chews.

FINISH: Extremely long, with hints of chocolate, nutmeg, and cinnamon

COMPARE THOUGHTS
Did this whiskey taste smooth for such a high proof?

YOUR TASTING NOTES:

EVAN WILLIAMS 1783

Kentucky Straight Bourbon Whiskey / Small Batch / Sour Mash

PROOF AND PRODUCT AGE: 86 proof. 6 years old.

BARRELS PER BOTTLING: 70 to 100

COLOR: Caramel

NOSE: Toasted almonds, hazelnut syrup, caramel, marshmallows, floral essence, and hints of vanilla and roasted cashews.

PALATE: The 1783 feels soft on the tongue and immediately meets the expectations of the nose. The toasted almonds, hazelnut syrup, and roasted cashew aromas turn into a Nutter Butter. The caramel and vanilla notes transform into a crème brûlée with a nice burnt and crispy surface. The chewy mouthfeel pleases throughout.

FINISH: Medium, with a tickle of nutmeg

COMPARE THOUGHTS
Did you pick up the Nutter Butter in the palate?

YOUR TASTING NOTES:

EVAN WILLIAMS BLACK LABEL

Kentucky Straight Bourbon Whiskey

PROOF AND PRODUCT AGE: 86 proof. No age statement, but it's roughly 5.5 years old.

BARRELS PER BOTTLING: 500 to 700

COLOR: Fairly dark for such a young bourbon, offering a near-full caramel color

NOSE: The nose is balanced with crème brûlée, vanilla, brown sugar, and a slight hint of cinnamon.

PALATE: The grains are slightly forward, but brown sugar and nutmeg quickly surface. It's a soft whiskey with a creamy mouthfeel and is quite lovely, bringing out all the patented notes of caramel and vanilla. This is one of my favorite starter bourbons for people just getting into bourbon.

FINISH: Medium and sweet

COMPARE THOUGHTS
What did you think of the color compared to similarly aged bourbons?

YOUR TASTING NOTES:

EVAN WILLIAMS SINGLE BARREL 2004
Single Barrel Vintage / Barrel no. 1 (barreled March 19, 2004) / Bottled November 16, 2013

PROOF AND PRODUCT AGE: 86.6 proof. The vintage indicates the year it was distilled, but these typically range between 9 and 10 years old.

BARRELS PER BOTTLING: 1

COLOR: Dark straw to russet

NOSE: Banana, pear, peach, pineapple juice, canned corn, lemon zest, and an array of caramels.

PALATE: The palate is warm, with a crispy mouthfeel. In addition to what's on the nose, ginger, nutmeg, and clove surface on the palate with hints of chocolate and spearmint.

FINISH: Medium with spice

COMPARE THOUGHTS
Did you get that hint of spearmint on the palate?

YOUR TASTING NOTES:

FIGHTING COCK
Kentucky Straight Bourbon Whiskey

PROOF AND PRODUCT AGE: 103 proof, 6 years old

BARRELS PER BOTTLING: 70 to 100

COLOR: Russet to brown

NOSE: Baked yams, toasted marshmallow, caramel, vanilla, and hints of spice.

PALATE: This bourbon is one of those for which the nose doesn't match the palate. The slightly astringent mouthfeel is off-putting but eventually dissipates. When the sensation leaves, the whiskey's intentions are realized, delivering caramel and spice.

FINISH: Short and briny

HENRY MCKENNA BOTTLED-IN-BOND

Kentucky Straight Bourbon Whiskey / Bottled-in-Bond / Barrel no. 1541 (filled May 4, 2004)

PROOF AND PRODUCT AGE: 100 proof. 10 years old.

BARRELS PER BOTTLING: 1

COLOR: Lighter cherry wood

NOSE: I've never found two Henry McKenna 10-year-olds that smell the same. That's the beauty of a single barrel—each product will vary from one before it, no matter how hard the distiller tries to keep them consistent. Barrel no. 1541 gives a first impression of licorice, cherries, and oak, completely catching me off-guard. Then, leather, pipe tobacco, and caramel set in, making me crave a sip of this masculine-smelling bourbon.

PALATE: Delicious canned black fruits, peaches, caramels, vanillas, spice, and hint of clove. Its chewy mouthfeel is a welcome delight and offers a lovely nutmeg toward the end.

FINISH: Long and spicy with nutmeg throughout

COMPARE THOUGHTS

Did you find the leather and pipe tobacco in the nose?

YOUR TASTING NOTES:

WILLETT FAMILY OF BRANDS

DISTILLERY: It's unknown for sure where the Willett products were distilled prior to 2012. Confidentiality contracts prohibit Willett from speaking about it, but most people surmise the whiskey originated from its neighbor, Heaven Hill. Whether Heaven Hill contract-distilled or sold bulk whiskey purchased from other distilleries is unknown. Wherever the bourbon originated, the whiskey was most certainly aged at the Willett warehouses.

MASTER DISTILLER: Father-and-son duo Even and Drew Kulsveen both distill and mingle.

MASHBILLS: For products distilled prior to 2012, the whiskey mashbills are unknown. Moving forward, the bourbon mashbills are:

> **BOURBON #1:** 72 percent corn, 13 percent rye, 15 percent Malt Barrel Entry with a barrel entry proof of 125

BOURBON #2: 65 percent corn, 20 percent wheat, and 15 percent malted barley with a barrel entry proof of 115

BOURBON #3: 52 percent corn, 38 percent rye, and 10 percent malted barley with a barrel entry proof of 125

BOURBON #4: 79 percent corn, 7 percent rye, and 14 percent malted barley with a barrel entry proof of 125

GRAIN ORIGINS: Corn and wheat come from Kentucky. The rye is purchased from the broker Brooks Grain in Minnesota. The barley is supplied from Malteurop.

DISTILLATION: The current Willett beer still was used in Juárez, Mexico, to make Mexican bourbon. The Willett doubler is a beauty symbol, shimmering in copper glory.

BARREL ENTRY PROOF: Unknown for products distilled prior to 2012. Post 2012 barrel-entry proofs are listed with the mashbills above.

FILTERING METHOD: The Willett Family Estate series is unfiltered, while the rest of the brands are chill filtered.

JOHNNY DRUM

Kentucky Straight Bourbon Whiskey / Private Stock

PROOF AND PRODUCT AGE: 101 proof. No age statement.

BARRELS PER BOTTLING: Unknown

FILTERING METHOD: Charcoal filtered

COLOR: Russet

NOSE: Dried apricot, strawberry jam, vanilla, caramel, and hints of coffee, tobacco, and cedar

PALATE: Warm and mouth-coating, this bourbon is similar to its sister bourbon—Willett Pot Still—and offers subtle complexities unfound in most bourbons. It's a marriage of delicious custards and subtle spices. No single thing stands out. From the caramels and spices to the vanillas and savory notes, Johnny Drum is balanced and complex with a beautiful nutmeg note rounding out the final moments.

FINISH: Long, with nutmeg

COMPARE THOUGHTS

Did you find this to be a complex bourbon?

YOUR TASTING NOTES:

NOAH'S MILL

Genuine Bourbon Whiskey / Batch QBC / Bottle no. 13-102

PROOF AND PRODUCT AGE: 114.3 proof. No age statement, but the bourbon includes barrels in the 15-year-old range. Due to the younger barrels in the batch, it's impossible to give an approximate average.

BARRELS PER BOTTLING: Fewer than 20

COLOR: Deep, dark amber

NOSE: Fresh-baked cornbread, cinnamon, ginger, plums, and cherry juice, followed by hints of caramel and baking spice.

PALATE: Edgy and hot, the dry mouthfeel is likely due to its higher proof, but it opens on the second taste with notes of crème brûlée, nutmeg, applesauce, and cinnamon-apple pie coming through.

FINISH: Short, with hints of baked apples

COMPARE THOUGHTS
Was your mouthfeel dry?

YOUR TASTING NOTES:

WILLETT POT STILL

Kentucky Straight Bourbon Whiskey / Bottle no. 250 of 274 from a single barrel (unidentifiable)

PROOF AND PRODUCT AGE: 94 proof. No age statement.

BARRELS PER BOTTLING: 1

COLOR: Light amber

NOSE: Beautiful and fruity with toasted oak, freshly crushed blueberries, burnt caramel, and vanilla bean extract. There's a slight smoke to this one.

PALATE: The complete palate offers a mouth-coating mouthfeel. No single note oversteps the other. In a word: it's balanced. But in the end the nose lends itself to the palate as it develops into vanilla custard with a nutmeg sprinkle on top, sweet cornbread with a

The Willett Distillery offers Kentucky one of the most picturesque bourbon facilities. It's family owned and offers rare and unique bourbons as well as rye whiskeys in the gift shop.

pat of salted butter, bread pudding with a drizzle of caramel sauce. Willett Pot Still, at least this bottle, is complex, changing from one taste to the next with a subtle champagne flavor quality to the final set of notes.

FINISH: Long, enduring, and complex

COMPARE THOUGHTS
It's rare to find a champagne-level of note in a bourbon. Did your bottle of Willett Pot Still feature this for you?

YOUR TASTING NOTES:

SELECT BUFFALO TRACE PRODUCTS: EAGLE RARE, GEORGE T. STAGG JR., AND OLD CHARTER

DISTILLERY: Buffalo Trace Distillery, Frankfort, Kentucky

MASTER DISTILLER: Harlen Wheatley

MASHBILL: Buffalo Trace does not disclose its mashbill but confirmed that these brands contain a "traditional mashbill," meaning the rye and malted barley are near equal parts in the recipe. Buffalo Trace calls this recipe its Mashbill #1.

GRAIN ORIGINS: Non-GMO corn comes from Kentucky and Indiana, while the rye originates from the Dakotas. All malted barley comes from North America.

DISTILLATION: Buffalo Trace products are double distilled on an 84-inch-wide column still and a doubler.

BARREL ENTRY PROOF: 125

AGING: Missouri Ozark American white oak with a char no. 4. Buffalo Trace's storied warehouses are labeled alphabetically and offer tremendous variety. For example, Warehouse K is a 9-story brick building with wooden floors, and Warehouse L is 5 stories and has concrete floors. K fluctuates greatly in temperature because of the generous airflow. In K, the first floor is cool and damp, which ages barrels more slowly, and the top is hot and dry, which ages them more quickly. Meanwhile, L experiences slower temperature changes thanks to its concrete and stores much of the distillery's wheated bourbons, including Pappy Van Winkle and Weller. For the company's limited-edition release Antique Collection, the distillery announces where the barrels are selected from, as if to reward the individual warehouse for the tremendous honor. Whiskeys for the mainstay products are stored throughout the compound. For the 2014 Antique Collection, George T. Stagg came from warehouses H, I, K, L, P, and Q; William Larue Weller from Warehouses D, K, and L; and Eagle Rare 17-year-old from Warehouses I and K. Suffice it to say, all these products were aged inside some legendary warehouses.

BARRELS PER BOTTLING: Unknown

FILTERING METHOD: Chill-filtered

BUFFALO TRACE
Kentucky Straight Bourbon Whiskey

PROOF AND PRODUCT AGE: 90 proof. No age statement, but the product ranges from 8 to 9 years old.

COLOR: Russet

NOSE: Vanilla, caramel, fresh-cut oak tree, baled hay, apricot, and a hint of rosemary

PALATE: The palate is filled with nutmeg spice and caramel, but the slightly snap-crackle-pop mouthfeel somewhat hides the custard and pumpkin notes. When they eventually show, the bourbon seems to run on all cylinders and offers up a slice of warm apple pie.

FINISH: Medium and spicy

COMPARE THOUGHTS
Did the notes take a while to develop on your palate?

YOUR TASTING NOTES:

EAGLE RARE
Kentucky Straight Bourbon Whiskey

PROOF AND PRODUCT AGE: 90 proof. 10 years old.

COLOR: Deep amber

NOSE: Gorgeous, with caramels, toffees, vanillas, and cinnamon stealing the show, but there's ample fruitcake, pies, and custard fillings entering the bouquet. Eagle Rare exemplifies a wonderful hazelnut note toward the end.

PALATE: Immediately, the bourbon coats the mouth, warming it all over for the perfect mouth-coating mouthfeel and delivering notes of pure bliss: pralines, crème brûlée, apple pie, pumpkin pie with nutmeg sprinkled on top, blueberry pie filling, and a cinnamon fire candy.

FINISH: Long and spicy

COMPARE THOUGHTS

Did your mouth instantly coat as soon as your tongue touched this bourbon?

YOUR TASTING NOTES:

In 1999, the George T. Stagg Distillery was renamed the Buffalo Trace Distillery. Since then, the facility has churned out some of the greatest whiskey of the past century.

GEORGE T. STAGG JR.

Kentucky Straight Bourbon Whiskey

PROOF AND PRODUCT AGE: 134.4 proof. No age statement, but ranges from 8 to 9 years old.

BARRELS PER BOTTLING: Small batches, but the number of barrels is not disclosed.

COLOR: Intense brown is to be expected. This bourbon is barrel proof, meaning it was extracted straight from the barrel and was not cut with water.

NOSE: Because it's barrel proof, the notes may be more difficult to pick up over the alcohol. Remember to open your mouth when nosing this beast. With my jaw extended, the whiskey aromas open up, bringing forth caramels, vanilla, nutmeg, cinnamon, and a unique spice rarely found in bourbon—Chinese allspice.

PALATE: For barrel proof, the bourbon sure is smooth, offering a raw sensation of grains right out of the gate, followed by the expected caramels and vanillas with a humming and resounding nutmeg that just warms the tongue. I also find the spices flourish toward the back of the tongue. As the high-proof bourbon gently trickles down the tongue, I score the mouthfeel in the creamy category and hope for a lingering finish.

FINISH: Alas, it's shorter than expected. The medium-spicy finish is smooth, but could be longer. I guess that's why this particular bourbon was selected for the "Jr." bottling.

COMPARE THOUGHTS
Did you taste Chinese allspice?

YOUR TASTING NOTES:

OLD CHARTER
Kentucky Straight Bourbon Whiskey

PROOF AND PRODUCT AGE: 80 proof. 8 years old.

COLOR: Light caramel. For an 8-year-old bourbon, this color is extremely light, even for an 80-proof bourbon. I expect more color from 8 years in the barrel.

NOSE: Floral notes, grain, cinnamon, caramel, and baking soda.

PALATE: Corn forward with rye and caramel-covered-popcorn notes. Slightly crisp mouthfeel gently gives warm nutmeg and cinnamon notes that become the resounding flavors in this whiskey.

FINISH: Very short, but good while it lasted

COMPARE THOUGHTS
Was this a short finish?

YOUR TASTING NOTES:

SELECT JIM BEAM PRODUCTS: BOOKER'S, BAKER'S, JIM BEAM BLACK, AND JIM BEAM WHITE

DISTILLERY: Jim Beam, Claremont, Kentucky, and Boston, Kentucky

MASTER DISTILLER: Fred Noe. Noe is the son of Booker Noe and is in more of an ambassador role these days.

MASHBILL: Jim Beam does not disclose its mashbill, but according to one obtained through the Oscar Getz Museum of Whiskey (which was included in a Jim Beam company report from the late 1970s), the mashbill for Jim Beam is 75 percent corn, 13 percent rye, and 12 percent malted barley. Other published Jim Beam mashbills indicate the rye level is 15 percent. Company officials confirm these percentages are "in the zone."

GRAIN ORIGINS: Corn comes from Indiana and rye comes from the Upper Midwest. The barley is grown in North Dakota, Montana, Idaho, Wyoming, and Colorado and malted in Minnesota and Wisconsin.

DISTILLATION: Double

BARREL ENTRY PROOF: 125

AGING: Jim Beam uses wood mostly from the Ozarks and aluminum-skinned warehouses. Barrels for the Booker's label tend to be on the higher floors, where the heat is just a little hotter in the summertime.

FILTERING METHOD: Chill filtration except for Booker's and Knob Creek Single Barrel

BOOKER'S
Kentucky Straight Bourbon Whiskey / Batch no. C07-B-7

PROOF AND PRODUCT AGE: 130.8 proof. (Note: Booker's varies in proof, so this number is specific to this particular bottle.) 7 years and 2 months old.

BARRELS PER BOTTLING: 375

COLOR: Dark brown to topsoil color

NOSE: Vibrant, floral, and fruity with caramel, vanilla, and rich, dark fruits.

PALATE: The proof shows up all right, and 2 eyedroppers of water are added to knock the heat down a little. After the water is added, the whiskey opens up with warm apple pie, pumpkin spice, nutmeg, gingerbread latté, crème brûlée, spicy rice cake, and vanilla custard.

Its mouth-coating mouthfeel is beautiful but would not be realized without a little water.

FINISH: Long and spicy

COMPARE THOUGHTS
Did you need to add water?

YOUR TASTING NOTES:

BAKER'S

Kentucky Straight Bourbon Whiskey / Batch no. B-90-001

PROOF AND PRODUCT AGE: 107 proof. 7 years old.

BARRELS PER BOTTLING: Unknown

COLOR: Russet

NOSE: The Baker's nose is always full of citrus, from lemon zest to fresh-squeezed orange juice. Oak and caramel accompany the citrus.

PALATE: Spice immediately hits in forms of fresh-cracked black pepper, cinnamon, and nutmeg, while the citrus follows. Baker's tends to offer a unique peppercorn flavor note that's savory and spicy at the same time.

FINISH: Medium, with spice

COMPARE THOUGHTS
Did you get the citrus?

YOUR TASTING NOTES:

JIM BEAM BLACK

Kentucky Straight Bourbon Whiskey

PROOF AND PRODUCT AGE: 86 proof. 6 to 8 years old. Jim Beam Black carried an age statement of 8 years until 2014, but the bottling no longer has this.

BARRELS PER BOTTLING: Unknown

COLOR: Light russet

Jim Beam is the number-one-selling bourbon. It's named after Colonel Beam, who purchased the Old Murphy Barber Distillery for his limestone rock business during Prohibition. When Prohibition ended and he could make bourbon again, Beam applied for distillery reinstatement and the facility was up and running.

NOSE: This is a raw, upfront nose with grains seemingly leading the charge, but really there's an earthiness to it, with notes of smoke and dirt and hints of caramel and vanilla.

PALATE: The palate is sweet with undertones of spice. The caramel and vanilla mingle with cornbread, mushrooms, and a lovely bread pudding with a dollop of whipped cream.

FINISH: Short, with a little touch of cinnamon

COMPARE THOUGHTS
Was Black earthy for you?

YOUR TASTING NOTES:

JIM BEAM WHITE
Kentucky Straight Bourbon Whiskey

PROOF AND PRODUCT AGE: 80 proof. No age statement, but averages 4 years old.

BARRELS PER BOTTLING: 700 to 800

COLOR: Straw

NOSE: Vanilla, lemon zest, pear, and hints of caramel and cinnamon.

PALATE: A crispy mouthfeel leads the way to simple notes of caramel and spice with unexpected hints of ginger and nutmeg.

FINISH: Short, with a touch of ginger

COMPARE THOUGHTS
Did you have a ginger in the finish?

YOUR TASTING NOTES:

OLD FORESTER SIGNATURE

Kentucky Straight Bourbon Whiskey

DISTILLERY: Brown-Forman Distillery, Shively, Kentucky

MASTER DISTILLER: Chris Morris

PROOF AND PRODUCT AGE: 100 proof. No age statement, but more than 4 years old.

MASHBILL: 72 percent corn, 18 percent rye, and 10 percent malted barley

GRAIN ORIGINS: Corn comes from Kentucky. Prior to 2013, most rye came from Canada. From then on, rye has originated from Europe. The malted barley comes from Montana.

DISTILLATION: Brown-Forman use two column stills—60-inch and another 48—and 2 thumpers.

BARREL ENTRY PROOF: 125

AGING: Old Forester barrels have been air-seasoned for an average of 6 months and charred to a no. 4 level. They're kept in climate-controlled warehouses.

BARRELS PER BOTTLING: 200

FILTERING METHOD: Carbon filtration

COLOR: Caramel

NOSE: Oh, for the money, this is one of the best noses in bourbon. It's layered in nutmeg, vanilla, caramel, honey, baking spices, and herbal notes that are just lovely.

PALATE: It's a slightly mouth-coating mouthfeel, warming the palate all over and delighting the senses with the notes found in the bouquet. The vanilla from the nose is now expressed more specifically as a custard, the caramel is the burnt crust atop a crème brûlée, and the spice is a rounded cinnamon note.

FINISH: Solid medium finish with hints of spice

COMPARE THOUGHTS

I was on the fence with Old Forester in the Nutmeg chapter because its nutmeg presence was about equal to vanilla and caramel, but it's still slightly more notable. How much nutmeg did you pick up?

YOUR TASTING NOTES:

CHAPTER SEVEN

CARAMEL-FORWARD
BOURBONS

Caramel. The sheer mention of this word, tantalizingly sweet, offers memories of soft caramel chews, caramel-slathered apples, chocolate candy bars with caramel nougat, caramel puddings, and other caramel joys that make the mouth salivate for confectionary delight. Every bourbon contains at least one measurable note of caramel. This is due to the charring technique, which caramelizes the barrel's wood sugars. But, inevitably, some bourbons pack more caramel than others.

Caramel-forward bourbons tend to go great with dessert. Any one of these products will taste delicious with a brownie.

Bourbons in the caramel-forward category tend to be nuanced and mouth coating, making them a true treat for sipping neat. The one common denominator: they frequently use wheat as the primary grain. In fact, I've found that while bourbons with high rye contents contain the patented caramel note, their spice dulls its caramel nuance. When made with lower amounts of rye or wheat, bourbon seems to blossom in caramel form many times over. It's worth noting that while this chapter is titled "Caramel-Forward Bourbons," one could make the argument for vanilla as a shared note, as it's as ever-present in many of these bourbons. But in my tasting studies, I've determined caramel is more pronounced, more nuanced, and more consistently prevalent. Of course, you'll need to taste—I mean study—for yourself.

BOURBON PUNCH

3 cups black tea, freshly brewed
3 cups ice
3 ounces spiced rum
3 ounces caramel-forward bourbon
1 ounce Mathilde Orange Liqueur
 au Cognac
1½ ounces orange juice
1 ounce lemon juice
2 teaspoons nutmeg
2 teaspoons cinnamon
One orange, thinly sliced

While you're steeping the tea, mix the ice, rum, whiskey, orange liqueur, and orange juice in a large punch bowl. Then, pour in the hot tea along with the lemon juice, nutmeg, and cinnamon. Stir until all the ice is dissolved. Add sliced oranges and serve.

MAKER'S MARK AND MAKER'S MARK BARREL STRENGTH

DISTILLERY: Maker's Mark, Loretto, Kentucky

MASTER DISTILLER: Greg Davis

MASHBILL: 70 percent corn, 16 percent soft red winter wheat, 14 percent malted barley

GRAIN ORIGINS: Corn and wheat are grown in the same county as the distillery. The malted barley comes from Milwaukee.

DISTILLATION: Maker's Mark uses 3 36-inch-wide column stills for its first distillation and a doubler for the second.

BARREL ENTRY PROOF: 110

AGING: Maker's Mark workhouse warehouses hold 50,000 barrels each. What's unique about them, though, is that workers rotate them from rick to rick. The theory is that this labor-intensive method ensures each barrel is exposed to the same temperatures over the course of its aging.

BARRELS PER BOTTLING: Varies, but most bottlings include 15 to 19.

MAKER'S MARK
Kentucky Straight Bourbon Whiskey

PROOF AND PRODUCT AGE: 90 proof. No age statement, but skews around 5 to 6 years.

FILTERING METHOD: Chill filtration

COLOR: Russet

NOSE: Maker's Mark has one of the classic noses among all of bourbon. It's consistently good, with notes of dried apricot, caramel, roasted corn, and vanilla as well as hints of chocolate and coffee.

PALATE: The enjoyable palate walks a fine line between balance and sophistication with notes of bread pudding, caramel-covered apples, vanilla custard, and a lovely pumpkin pie. The creamy mouthfeel leaves you wanting more.

FINISH: Medium, with a subtle cinnamon note

COMPARE THOUGHTS

Pumpkin pie is perhaps the one note in Maker's Mark I find signature to the brand. It's not that pumpkin pie doesn't exist in other bourbons; it just stands out in Maker's. Did you find this note?

YOUR TASTING NOTES:

MAKER'S MARK BARREL STRENGTH
Batch no. 14-01

PROOF AND PRODUCT AGE: 113 proof. No age statement, but around 6 years old.

FILTERING METHOD: Uncut and unfiltered

COLOR: Deep russet with gold hues

NOSE: The nose is certainly an indication of a much higher proof than traditional Maker's Mark. This bourbon's alcohol content makes itself known rather quickly and almost hides the beautiful caramel, marshmallow, and vanilla notes. The bouquet continues to express itself with fresh-baked apple pie and a hint of cinnamon. But make no mistake about this bourbon—the main note is caramel.

PALATE: All the beauty of the bouquet appears on the tongue, tickling with pronounced caramel and vanilla in form of custards, pie fillings, and even a buttery, fresh-baked pumpkin pie with whipped cream on top. This bourbon certainly offers a lot, giving a range of spices—from allspice to cinnamon and nutmeg—quickly after the pumpkin.

FINISH: Long and lovely, with a hint of apple pie

COMPARE THOUGHTS

Yum. Who knew apple pie on the finish could be so lovely? Please tell me you got that, too.

YOUR TASTING NOTES:

Renowned glass artist Dale Chihuly created this special display in a Maker's Mark warehouse. The distillery is beautiful by itself, but the glasswork is a sight for the ages. It also represents how bourbon distillers are adding onto the visitor experience—when Marjorie Samuels pioneered the idea of a Maker's Mark visitor attraction, nobody could predict that a world-renowned artist would craft such beauty inside a warehouse.

LARCENY

Kentucky Straight Bourbon Whiskey

DISTILLERY: Heaven Hill Bernheim, Louisville, Kentucky

MASTER DISTILLER: Craig Beam

PROOF AND PRODUCT AGE: 92 proof. No age statement, but the brand uses barrels between 6 years old and 12 years old.

MASHBILL: 68 percent corn, 20 percent wheat, 12 percent malted barley

GRAIN ORIGINS: Corn comes from Southern Indiana and Kentucky. The red winter wheat is produced in Kentucky, while the barley is grown in the Dakotas and Washington but is malted in Wisconsin.

DISTILLATION: Double distilled in the same equipment outlined for Evan Williams on page 141.

BARREL ENTRY PROOF: 125

AGING: Barrels are made from American white oak from mostly the Ozark region, made at the Independent Stave Company or McGinnis Cooperage with a no. 3 char. Bourbon is aged in Bardstown, Kentucky, warehouses. Larceny is selected from open-rick warehouses, floors 4 through 6.

BARRELS PER BOTTLING: 70 to 100

FILTERING METHOD: Chill filtration

COLOR: Russet

NOSE: Fully floral, almost like walking into a garden of lilies, roses, and honeysuckle vines. From here, it's your typical bourbon notes—caramel, several vanilla layers, and a resounding toasted almond.

PALATE: The mouthfeel leans toward crispy and dry, with powerful vanilla cake batter and fudge brownies with nuts offering the first notes on the palate. The more delicate notes are found toward the middle of the tongue and include an assortment of fruits and caramel. There's just a hint of spice toward the end.

FINISH: Medium, with a lovely note of nutmeg

COMPARE THOUGHTS

Was the nose floral?

YOUR TASTING NOTES:

WELLER SPECIAL RESERVE
Kentucky Straight Bourbon Whiskey

DISTILLERY: Buffalo Trace, Frankfort, Kentucky

MASTER DISTILLER: Harlen Wheatley

PROOF AND PRODUCT AGE: 90 proof. No age statement; the W. L. Weller Special Reserve once carried an age statement of 7 years old, but this was dropped in recent years. However, the whiskey still averages 7 years old, according to the distiller.

MASHBILL: Wheated bourbon. The Buffalo Trace Distillery will not disclose its mashbills, and previously published grain percentages have not been confirmed as accurate. However, company officials indicate that Buffalo Trace's wheated-bourbon mashbill is within a few percentage points of 70 percent corn, 16 percent wheat, and 14 percent malted barley.

GRAIN ORIGINS: All corn for Weller products is non-GMO and comes from Kentucky and Indiana. The wheat originates from North Dakota, South Dakota, and Minnesota.

DISTILLATION: Double distilled as outlined in Buffalo Trace on page 148.

BARREL ENTRY PROOF: 114

AGING: Weller has historically used Missouri-based American white oak to make barrels for all Buffalo Trace products, but wood shortages have led to the company purchasing barrel wood from surrounding states.

BARRELS PER BOTTLING: Unknown

FILTERING METHOD: Chill filtration

COLOR: Russet

NOSE: Lovely nose of fruits, caramel, watermelon candies, and fresh-baked bread.

PALATE: For the money, this is a great palate, but if money were not a factor, I'd have to say that this palate burns in the beginning a little too much for my liking and opens up a slightly dry mouthfeel. When the burn ends, however, the caramel and vanilla notes truly open up and the watermelon candy expresses itself in the form of one of my favorite childhood candies—watermelon Jolly Ranchers.

FINISH: Very short

Did you find a burn in the beginning?

YOUR TASTING NOTES:

W. L. WELLER 12 YEAR

Kentucky Straight Bourbon Whiskey

PROOF AND PRODUCT AGE: 90 proof. 12 years old.

BARRELS PER BOTTLING: Unknown

FILTERING METHOD: Chill filtration

COLOR: Deep amber

NOSE: This nose is what whiskey dreams are made of. It's a classic walk with rose petals, freshly cut grass, caramel, vanilla, peach cobbler, apple pie, and freshly crushed dark cherries.

PALATE: The palate picks up where the nose left off. I love that! It's soft and gentle, showing no sign of alcohol burn whatsoever, and delivers a creamy mouthfeel with hints of pear. There is more of that peach cobbler and apple pie, but it really packs a resounding hit of the vanilla and caramel. The cinnamon picked up in this bourbon is found on the tip of the tongue, as opposed the back like many other cinnamon notes in bourbon.

FINISH: Long and balanced, with caramel and vanilla

COMPARE THOUGHTS
Wasn't the nose an absolute treat?

YOUR TASTING NOTES:

WELLER ANTIQUE 107
Kentucky Straight Bourbon Whiskey

PROOF AND PRODUCT AGE: 107 proof. No age statement.

BARRELS PER BOTTLING: Unknown

FILTRATION: Chill filtration

COLOR: Tawny

NOSE: Whipped cream, caramel, vanilla, oak, and dark cherry juice.

PALATE: And so begins the journey of a higher-proof bourbon that could be lost in the alcohol content. Fortunately, this lovely product finds the balance between proof and flavor. The notes on the nose surface on the palate quickly and add a slew of other notes, including roasted almonds, a slice of grilled tofu, apples, and cinnamon.

FINISH: Medium, with a resounding note of a pumpkin-spice latté.

COMPARE THOUGHTS
My finish on Weller Antique 107 is very specific. Did you find pumpkin spice latté anywhere in this bourbon?

YOUR TASTING NOTES:

MICHTER'S US 1
Bourbon Whiskey / Small Batch / Batch no. 7414536

DISTILLERY: Prior to fall 2015, Michter's did not produce its own whiskey, instead contract-distilling its recipes with Brown-Forman in Shively, Kentucky. Today, however, the maker distills its own whiskey.

MASTER DISTILLER: Willie Pratt is the master distiller. Pamela Heilmann is the company's vice president of operations and was formerly a distiller at Jim Beam's Booker Noe Distillery in Boston, Kentucky.

PROOF AND PRODUCT AGE: 91.4 proof. No age statement.

MASHBILL: 79 percent corn, 11 percent rye, 10 percent malted barley

GRAIN ORIGINS: Unknown

DISTILLATION: Michter's new column still is 32 inches in diameter. It uses both a thumper and doubler.

BARREL ENTRY PROOF: 103

AGING: All Michter's barrels are aged in climate-controlled warehouses. The company negotiates barrel placement in contracted warehouses.

BARRELS PER BOTTLING: Fewer than 24

FILTERING METHOD: Michter's is something of a filtration house, using three types of chill filtration: plate-and-frame, canister, and sparkler. The company filters each product differently. In an experiment with filtration systems, Michter's once filtered a rye whiskey 32 different ways.

COLOR: Russet

NOSE: Light aromas of floral essence and fruits, with delicious, mouthwatering notes of caramel, toasted pecans, oak, and vanilla extract as well as hints of pine and pear.

PALATE: This is a soft bourbon with a creamy mouthfeel, so doesn't sting but takes a little more time for the flavors to develop. Once they do, you'll find the patented caramels and vanillas, but this also has a lovely chocolate and cinnamon flavor combined into one note.

FINISH: Medium, with doses of cinnamon chocolate

COMPARE THOUGHTS

Cinnamon chocolate is not your everyday note. Did you get this?

YOUR TASTING NOTES:

Once produced in Pennsylvania, Michter's now operates in Kentucky. Up until 2015, the brand either purchased sourced whiskey or contract-distilled. Moving forward, this still will make all Michter's.

WOODFORD RESERVE DISTILLER'S SELECT
Batch no. 960 / Bottle no. 1842

DISTILLERY: Woodford Reserve Distillery in Versailles, Kentucky, and Brown-Forman Distillery in Shively, Kentucky. Distillations from these two facilities are mingled in batches to create Woodford Reserve; the exact percentages are unknown.

MASTER DISTILLER: Chris Morris

PROOF AND PRODUCT AGE: 90.4 proof. No age statement, but tends to be around 7 years old.

MASHBILL: 72 percent corn, 18 percent rye; 10 percent malted barley

GRAIN ORIGINS: Non-GMO corn comes from Kentucky, rye came from Canada prior to 2012 and now comes from Europe. Malted barley comes from the Dakotas.

DISTILLATION: Distillations at the Woodford Reserve Distillery are triple distilled, but those at Brown-Forman are double distilled.

BARREL ENTRY PROOF: 125

AGING: Brown-Forman is the only whiskey company that owns its own cooperages and thus has greater access to barrel wood than other distilleries and at lesser cost. Woodford Reserve barrels are made from American white oak wood, mostly originating in Kentucky and Tennessee, and contain a char no. 4. They're stored in climate-controlled warehouses.

BARRELS PER BOTTLING: 130

FILTERING METHOD: Carbon filtration

COLOR: Deep amber

NOSE: Woodford Reserve offers a beautiful nose of mango, apples, caramels, vanillas, cinnamon, toffee, blueberry pie, and oak.

PALATE: The warm palate is straight out of a Christmas movie, with notes of nutmeg, cinnamon, eggnog, pumpkin pie, caramel, vanilla, gingerbread, and baking spice. There's a beautiful smoky note in this bourbon, too, which reminds me of Texas barbecue.

FINISH: Long and spicy

COMPARE THOUGHTS
Does this bourbon taste like Christmas to you?

YOUR TASTING NOTES:

WOODFORD RESERVE DOUBLE OAKED
Kentucky Straight Bourbon Whiskey

PROOF AND PRODUCT AGE: 90.4 proof. No age statement, but it is between 7 and 8 years old.

BARREL ENTRY PROOF: Before the traditional Woodford Reserve is dumped into new barrels, it's cut with water to 97 proof and then placed in the second new charred oak barrel.

AGING: The Double Oaked product takes existing Woodford Reserve, cuts it, and dumps it into a new barrel that has undergone a long toasting method, which is a less concentrated flame than charring, and finished with a light charring. The intent is to extract sweet oak character that might be lost in longer chars. The whiskey then sits inside the new barrels for an additional year.

BARRELS PER BOTTLING: 50

FILTERING METHOD: Carbon filtration

COLOR: This is the darkest product under 10 years old you'll ever find. The extra barrel gives Double Oak the richest deep amber in bourbon.

NOSE: Screams desserts, from chocolates to honey and caramel, raspberry and blueberry pie to dark cherry jam. The bouquet is sweet, without a hint of spice.

PALATE: Picks up the dessert trend and becomes a chocolate pie filling or pudding with additional notes of honey, caramel, Hershey's chocolate bar, and raspberry jam. Toward the end, citrus, specifically a slight lemony flavor, enters the conversation and offers a lovely crispy mouthfeel.

FINISH: Medium, with hints of orange chocolate

COMPARE THOUGHTS
Did this taste like dessert to you?

YOUR TASTING NOTES:

Cinnamon-forward bourbons tend to offer more rye in the mashbill, but that's not a steadfast rule. Maker's 46 is a wheated bourbon, but gleans spice from the French oak staves used to produce the whiskey.

CHAPTER EIGHT
CINNAMON-FORWARD
BOURBONS

When Mom hung our family spice rack in the kitchen, as a young boy with a palate eager to taste, there was one bottle I grabbed and sprinkled over everything from eggs to hot dogs: cinnamon. The first time I remember tasting this spice it was in the form of a cinnamon toothpick my baseball pal made with his dad. It was hot and fiery, warm and sweet, and tickly and earthy. Quite simply, with an undeveloped palate at ten years old, I found cinnamon to be exciting, breaking away from the boring ketchup, salt, and pepper, which were the only ingredients I understood at that age.

Today, cinnamon remains a beloved ingredient in my life and is a beautiful tasting note in many high-rye bourbons. After it's cooked, fermented, and distilled, rye expresses itself as spicy. But rye is not an automatic cinnamon-note deliverer. In rye whiskey, which is its own category that requires at least 51 percent rye in the mashbill, cinnamon is not as common as it is in higher-rye bourbons. These bourbons offer the perfect marriage between corn and rye to create the beautiful cinnamon note.

But as you will see, there's more than one way to get the spice.

MAKER'S 46

Kentucky Bourbon Whiskey

DISTILLERY: Maker's Mark Distillery, Loretto, Kentucky

MASTER DISTILLER: Greg Davis

PROOF AND PRODUCT AGE: 94 proof. No age statement, but around 6 years old.

MASHBILL: Same as Maker's Mark (see page 161)

AGING: French oak staves are added to existing barrels. Since French oak contains 9 times the tannic acid as American oak, adding these staves is intended to spice up the whiskey.

COLOR: Light straw to light caramel. Very light for something with so much time in the barrel.

NOSE: Beautiful—a merriment of freshly picked flowers, caramel, vanilla, and black fruits. There's a slight hint of cinnamon in some bottles, but this note is inconsistent in Maker's 46. Sometimes you nose cinnamon, sometimes you don't.

PALATE: My first thought is this isn't Maker's Mark at all. It's spicy and laden with dark fruits, with a somewhat dry mouthfeel. I also get the vanilla and caramel expressed in the nose. But the French oak staves did their job; spice wins. However, I recommend buying 2 bottles and tasting them side by side. As single barrels often do, each Maker's 46 tastes different.

FINISH: The medium finish is slightly smooth, although there's a gentle tickle down the pipe.

COMPARE THOUGHTS

What did you think of the color compared to other bourbons around the same age? Compare Maker's 46 to regular Maker's Mark—notice a difference?

YOUR TASTING NOTES:

Every bottle at the Maker's Mark Distillery is hand-dipped in its patented red wax. This was one of the first bottles of Maker's 46 to be dipped.

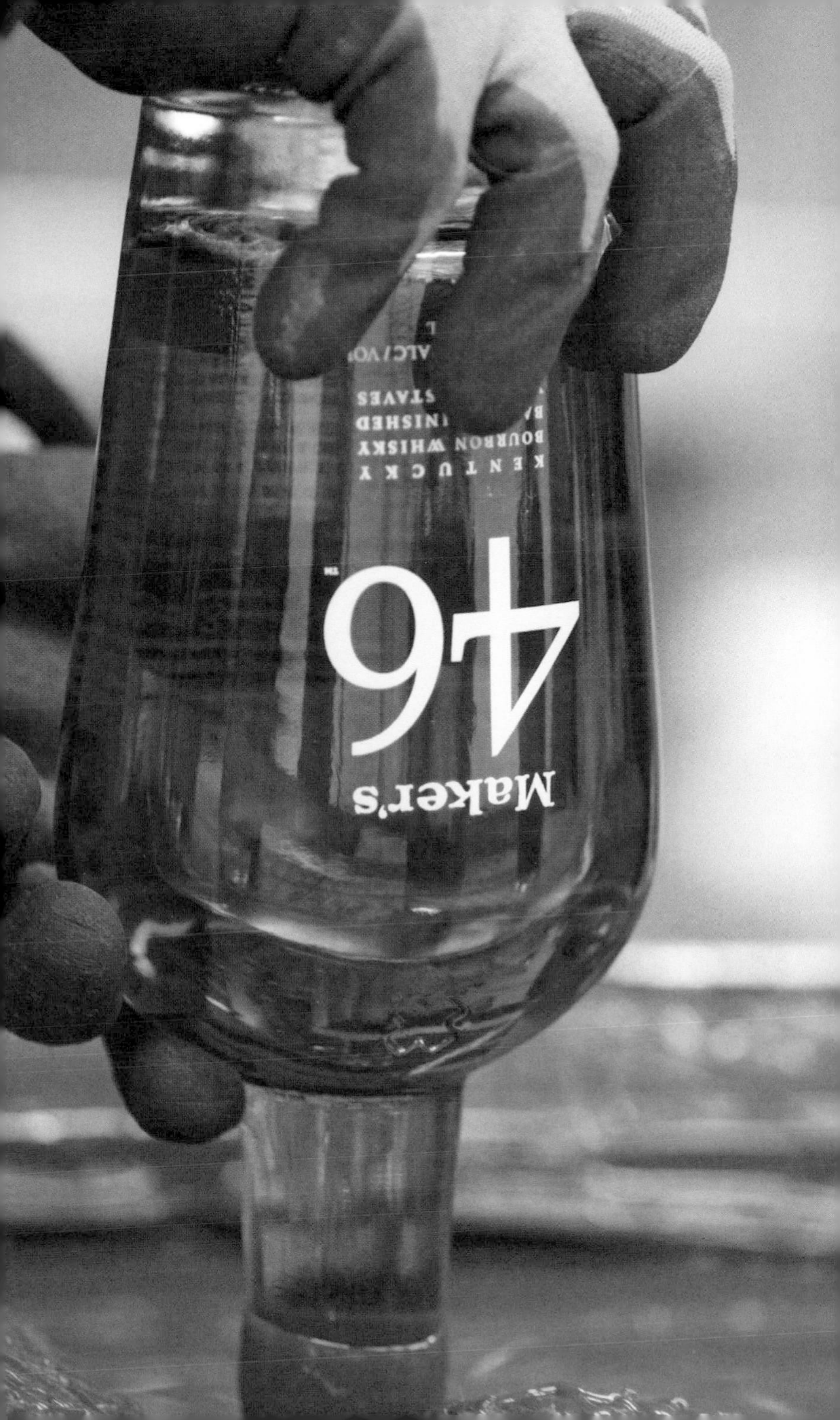
Maker's
46
KENTUCKY
BOURBON WHISKY
STAVES

SELECT BUFFALO TRACE PRODUCTS: BLANTON'S AND ROCK HILL

Kentucky Straight Bourbon Whiskey / Single Barrel

DISTILLERY: Buffalo Trace Distillery, Frankfort, Kentucky

MASTER DISTILLER: Harlen Wheatley

PROOF AND PRODUCT AGE: 90 proof. 9 years old.

MASHBILL: Medium rye mashbill, which means that the rye is usually 5 to 10 percentage points higher than the barley. A mashbill of 75 percent corn, 15 percent rye, and 10 percent malted barley would be considered in the medium-rye mashbill category. Buffalo Trace calls this Mashbill #2.

GRAIN ORIGINS: Corn comes from Kentucky and Indiana, rye from the Dakotas.

DISTILLATION: Double (see page 148)

BARREL ENTRY PROOF: 125

BARRELS PER BOTTLING: 1

FILTERING METHOD: Chill filtration

COLOR: Russet

NOSE: Love the nose. Cherry blossoms, canned fruits, dried apricot, and a lovely combination of vanilla and caramel with toffee and cocoa. It's just a beautiful nose.

PALATE: The caramel and vanilla combination joins chocolate, cinnamon, and pepper to form a single taste similar to Mexican cinnamon chocolates. A mouth-coating mouthfeel warms the palate throughout.

FINISH: Long and spicy

COMPARE THOUGHTS
How would you classify the spice in this bourbon?

YOUR TASTING NOTES:

FIG AND BOURBON

1 fig
1½ ounces fresh sour mix
Pinch of ground nutmeg
½ ounce orange curacao
1½ ounces bourbon

The fig is paramount to this recipe. If you can't find a good fig, well, the cocktail won't work. Thinly slice your fig and set aside a piece for garnish. Use the rest to muddle with the sour mix in the shaker—bring the sour and fig together in cocktail shaker matrimony. Add the rest of the ingredients with ice and shake until frost forms on the shaker. Strain into glass and garnish with fig.

ROCK HILL FARMS
Kentucky Straight Bourbon Whiskey / Single Barrel

PROOF AND PRODUCT AGE: 100 proof. No age statement, but tends to be around 10 years old.

COLOR: Deep amber

NOSE: Dried berries, tobacco, spice, cherry pie, caramel, toffee, and vanilla.

PALATE: Mouth-coating mouthfeel. Chocolate and pumpkin pie, the notes on the nose, and a resounding spice—perhaps a cinnamon-and-nutmeg combination—really bring this bourbon home. The final flavor seems to be a smoky, almost briny, quality that might be construed as peat by veteran Scotch drinkers.

FINISH: Long and smoky

COMPARE THOUGHTS
Did you detect the unique smoke in this?

YOUR TASTING NOTES:

BLANTON'S
Barrel no. 599 (dumped May 21, 2014)

PROOF AND PRODUCT AGE: 93 proof. No age statement, but Blanton's skews between 6 and 8 years old.

AGING: Missouri American white oak barrels with a char no. 4, aged in the center of Buffalo Trace's Warehouse H. The bottle I tasted was no. 136 on the Blanton master registrar, a list the distillery keeps of every Blanton's produced.

BARRELS PER BOTTLING: 1

FILTERING METHOD: Chill filtration

COLOR: Deep amber

NOSE: Rich, filled with oodles of caramels, vanillas, spices, dried apricot, cherry-flavored pipe tobacco, cigar box, saddle leather, and oak.

PALATE: Beautiful and fruit forward with the essence of everything found in the bouquet. The creamy mouthfeel, almost like dripping butter, coats the tongue with notes of cinnamon, crème brûlée, pumpkin pie, and delicious mashed yams with brown sugar and butter. This bourbon also shows hints of chocolate and baking spices.

FINISH: Long, spicy, and delightful

COMPARE THOUGHTS

The nose was laden with masculine notes of tobacco, leather, and cigar box. Did you pick this up?

YOUR TASTING NOTES:

A. SMITH BOWMAN SMALL BATCH
Virginia Straight Bourbon Whiskey / Small Batch

DISTILLERY: The first distillate comes from Buffalo Trace, which double distills it at the A. Smith Bowman Distillery in Fredericksburg, Virginia.

MASTER DISTILLER: Truman Cox was distiller for this product. He passed away in February 2013, and Brian Prewitt became the master distiller shortly thereafter.

PROOF AND PRODUCT AGE: 90 proof. No age statement, but it is 6 years old.

MASHBILL: Same as Buffalo Trace (see page 148)

GRAIN ORIGINS: Same as Buffalo Trace (see page 148)

DISTILLATION: Triple

BARREL ENTRY PROOF: 125

AGING: A. Smith Bowman barrels are made of Missouri Ozark American white oak and feature a 3.5-level char. The barrels age standing upright and are stacked upon pallets versus the rick system used in Kentucky.

BARRELS PER BOTTLING: Unknown

FILTERING METHOD: Chill filtration

COLOR: Light brown

NOSE: With its floral and fruity base, this whiskey smells close to perfume. But the patented notes of caramel and vanilla shine through, reminding you that this is no perfume; it's certainly bourbon.

PALATE: The palate tastes drastically different from the Buffalo Trace products, leading one to believe that Virginia's whiskey is night and day compared with Kentucky's. The palate is warm, with a creamy mouthfeel that brings forth notes of cinnamon, nutmeg, pumpkin, caramel, and apple pie.

FINISH: Long, with hints of cinnamon

COMPARE THOUGHTS
Did the nose come off as perfumelike to you?

YOUR TASTING NOTES:

BULLEIT BOURBON
Kentucky Straight Bourbon Whiskey

DISTILLERY: Bulleit was distilled at Four Roses until the two companies parted ways in the spring of 2014, around the same time Diageo announced a $115 million Bulleit distillery in Shelby County, Kentucky. Until this distillery is completed, Bulleit contract-distills with unknown facilities.

MASTER DISTILLER: Unknown. Bulleit founder Tom Bulleit (pronounced "bullet") is not the distiller, but he's a great salesman! A master distiller has not yet been named for the brand's new facility.

PROOF AND PRODUCT AGE: 90 proof. No age statement, but bottlings contain bourbon around 6 years old.

MASHBILL: 68 percent corn, 28 percent rye, 4 percent malted barley

GRAIN ORIGINS: Indiana and Kentucky for the corn, Midwest for the barley, and Europe for the rye

BARREL ENTRY PROOF: 125

AGING: The barrel wood comes from Missouri and the Appalachian states. Currently, Bulleit Bourbon is aged at the Stitzel-Weller Distillery warehouses in Shively; once the new distillery is up in Shelby County, expect Bulleit to be mostly aged there.

BARRELS PER BOTTLING: Unknown

FILTERING METHOD: Chill filtration

COLOR: Caramel with a slight tint on the edges

NOSE: Spicy with floral and fruit. Bulleit always smells to me as if there's a slight hint of a French perfume store deep inside.

PALATE: Grain and caramel express themselves almost simultaneously, but an overwhelming baking spice comes through quickly, and citrus and caramel carom off the tongue. Mouthfeel is slightly astringent.

FINISH: Short to medium and full of spice

COMPARE THOUGHTS
Did you find the alluring perfume nose?

YOUR TASTING NOTES:

1792 RIDGEMONT RESERVE AND VERY OLD BARTON
1792 RIDGEMONT RESERVE
Kentucky Straight Bourbon Whiskey

DISTILLERY: 1792 Barton

MASTER DISTILLER: Ken Pierce

PROOF AND PRODUCT AGE: 93.7 proof. No age statement, but ranges from 8 to 9 years old.

MASHBILL: High-rye bourbon, meaning the rye is between 28 and 35 percent of the mashbill.

GRAIN ORIGINS: Indiana and Kentucky for corn. Rye comes from the Dakotas and the malted barley from throughout North America.

DISTILLATION: 1792 Barton's uses a 72-inch-wide column still and a doubler.

BARREL ENTRY PROOF: 125

AGING: Barton uses Missouri white oak barrels with a char no. 3.5 for 1792. The barrels are aged in Warehouse Z at their facility.

BARRELS PER BOTTLING: Unknown

FILTERING METHOD: Chill filtration

COLOR: Russet

NOSE: Burnt corn on the cob, caramel, vanilla, cinnamon bread, oak, and leather.

PALATE: The bourbon is smoky with all the lovely notes on the nose, but especially caramel and vanilla with hints of cinnamon. It also shows elements of bell pepper, toasted almonds, banana, and hints of citrus. It features a mouth-coating, velvety mouthfeel.

FINISH: Medium, with hints of banana

COMPARE THOUGHTS
Did the whiskey express bell pepper for you?

YOUR TASTING NOTES:

VERY OLD BARTON
Kentucky Straight Bourbon Whiskey

PROOF AND PRODUCT AGE: 90 proof. No age statement. Very Old Barton used to carry an age statement of 6 years but no longer does; the bourbon is around 5 years old today.

COLOR: Light straw

NOSE: A very earthy nose with rustic metal smells and smoke. I pick up spice, vanilla, and just a slight hint of caramel.

PALATE: The palate is much less expressive than the nose would suggest. The alcohol burn for this low of a proof is disconcerting and overshadows a slightly dry mouthfeel. Eventually, I'm able to taste the grains, bubble gum, and cinnamon.

FINISH: Extremely short

COMPARE THOUGHTS
Bubble gum is not the most common note. Did you pick it up?

YOUR TASTING NOTES:

OLD GRAND DAD 114
Kentucky Straight Bourbon Whiskey / Lot no. 1

DISTILLERY: Jim Beam

PROOF AND PRODUCT AGE: 114 proof. No age statement.

MASHBILL: High-rye mashbill, with the rye accounting for about 27 percent to 30 percent of the recipe. For other technical specs, see Jim Beam on page 153.

COLOR: Russet

NOSE: Earthy, featuring fresh-cut tree branch, slight pine, cornbread, maple syrup, and caramel.

PALATE: Very grain forward, but the grains are mature and cooked, perhaps in the form of cornbread or a stew; this bourbon is a sure-fire winner if you love your grains. After the raw and earthy notes subside, caramel and vanilla set in, followed by an overpowering cinnamon that sticks to the end with a dry mouthfeel.

FINISH: Medium, with cinnamon-dusted apples

COMPARE THOUGHTS
Did the grains appeal to you?

YOUR TASTING NOTES:

Knob Creek Single Barrel sits on a porch with a snowy Jim Beam Distillery backdrop. There's nothing quite like enjoying a nip of bourbon on a cold, snowy day.

KNOB CREEK SINGLE BARREL RESERVE

Kentucky Straight Bourbon Whiskey / Small Batch / Single Barrel Reserve
(seems redundant to include small batch and single barrel, but hey, that's what
they put on the label)

DISTILLERY: Jim Beam

PROOF AND PRODUCT AGE: 120 proof. 9 years old.

MASHBILL, GRAIN ORIGINS, AND DISTILLATION: See tech specs with Jim Beam products on page 153.

FILTERING METHOD: Non–chill filtration

COLOR: Deep amber

NOSE: This nose reminds me of my youth. Filled with the sweet feed I used to give my horses, it is reminiscent of so many wonderful farm smells without evoking the bad ones. There's fresh-cut grass, clove, barbecue smoke, and a dose of caramel that won't quit.

PALATE: This is too smooth for 120 proof. I had to double-check the bottle, because I felt an array of gorgeous caramel, vanilla, and fruit notes hit my tongue before I even detected a hint of burn. The spice that follows expresses itself in the form of baking spices as opposed to black pepper spices, and it shows just how complex a higher-proof bourbon can be.

FINISH: Medium, with vanilla custard

COMPARE THOUGHTS
Was this high-proof bourbon smooth for you?

YOUR TASTING NOTES:

WILD TURKEY PRODUCTS

DISTILLERY: Wild Turkey Distillery, Lawrenceburg, Kentucky

MASTER Distillers: Jimmy and Eddie Russell

MASHBILL: 75 percent corn, 13 percent rye, and 12 percent malted barley. Wild Turkey does not disclose its mashbills, but company officials say this frequently cited recipe was "close."

GRAIN ORIGINS: All grains are non-GMO and mostly sourced from Kentucky farmers. Rye comes from Germany, while malted barley is from the Dakotas.

DISTILLATION: Wild Turkey double distills using a 60-inch-by-52-foot-tall column still with 19 stripping plates and a 28,595-gallon doubler.

BARREL ENTRY PROOF: 114 proof

FILTERING METHOD: Chill filtration

WILD TURKEY 101
Kentucky Straight Bourbon Whiskey

PROOF AND PRODUCT AGE: 101 proof. No age statement, but skews toward 8 years old.

BARRELS PER BOTTLING: 1,200 to 1,300

COLOR: Russet

NOSE: Wild Turkey 101 always brings a juicy nose, offering up aromas of fresh-squeezed cherry, orange, and even kiwi juices. This is followed by a bouquet of heavy spice, from black pepper to cayenne, which permeates to the very end and almost overpowers the caramel.

PALATE: The spice continues, but it is much less pronounced here and doesn't overpower the creamy mouthfeel and delicate notes of chocolate, caramel, and vanilla custard. I find the juice notes on the nose are now fully cooked apples and peach cobbler with cinnamon dust on top.

FINISH: Short, with a hint of cinnamon

COMPARE THOUGHTS
How about that nose? Did you find it to be juicy?

YOUR TASTING NOTES:

There are legends and then there is longtime Wild Turkey master distiller Jimmy Russell, who is the friendliest and kindest fella in the business. He's worked at the distillery for more than sixty years.

WILD TURKEY RARE BREED
Kentucky Straight Bourbon Whiskey / Barrel Proof / Batch no. WT-03RB

PROOF AND PRODUCT AGE: 108.2 proof (this product ranges in from around 108 to 114 proof). No age statement.

COLOR: Deep amber

NOSE: Ultraspicy with notes of jalapeño, cracked black pepper, and traditional baking spices. The caramel note is more that of a caramel syrup used in coffees. The vanilla is sharp, like vanilla extract.

PALATE: Extraordinarily smooth and light for such high proof, with spice throughout and crème brûlée, cherry pie filling, and powerful notes of nutmeg and cinnamon.

FINISH: Medium, with cinnamon

COMPARE THOUGHTS
Did you get the jalapeño?

YOUR TASTING NOTES:

RUSSELL'S RESERVE 10-YEAR-OLD SMALL BATCH
Kentucky Straight Bourbon Whiskey

PROOF AND PRODUCT AGE: 90 proof. 10 years old.

BARRELS PER BOTTLING: Unknown

COLOR: Light amber

NOSE: Oak, blackberry, barbecue smoke, refried beans, spent coffee grounds, caramel, and cinnamon.

PALATE: This is an old-school-tasting bourbon with a mouthfeel that drips down to the very bottom of your tongue and coats every inch from cheek to cheek. It's uniquely complex, with berry notes, apple, caramel chews, custard, and a savory Mexican dish, perhaps a hot tamale with a red chili sauce.

FINISH: Long and spicy

COMPARE THOUGHTS
Did you get the savory Mexican dish on the end?

YOUR TASTING NOTES:

FOUR ROSES FAMILY

DISTILLERY: Four Roses, Lawrenceburg, Kentucky

MASTER DISTILLER: Jim Rutledge

MASHBILL: Four Roses uses 10 recipes that are represented on the labels using 4 letters that each represent something pertinent to the distillery.

> O = Produced at the Four Roses Distillery
>
> E = Mashbill is 75 percent corn, 20 percent rye, 5 percent malted barley
>
> B = Mashbill is 60 percent corn, 35 percent rye, 5 percent malted barley
>
> S = Straight whiskey distillation

Additional letters indicate the yeast strain used during fermentation. V is light fruit; Q is floral essences; K is spicy, with nutmeg and cinnamon; O is fruity with hints of milk stout; F is herbal essences.

GRAIN ORIGINS: Corn is from Indiana and Kentucky. Rye is from Europe.

DISTILLATION: Double

BARREL ENTRY PROOF: 120

AGING: Missouri to Kentucky American white oak barrels with a char no. 4, stored in single-story warehouses

BARRELS PER BOTTLING: 1 for Single Barrel, 150 for Four Roses Yellow Label, and 180 for Four Roses Small Batch

FILTERING METHOD: Chill filtration

FOUR ROSES YELLOW LABEL
Kentucky Straight Bourbon Whiskey

PROOF AND PRODUCT AGE: 80 proof. No age statement, but averages 5 to 6 years.

MASHBILL: Uses all 10 Four Roses recipes (see above)

BARRELS PER BOTTLING: 150

Four Roses master distiller Jim Rutledge once attempted to buy the company from its then parent company Seagram's. At the time, Four Roses was only sold overseas, and Rutledge wanted the brand back in the United States. He eventually got his wish under a new parent company and led one of the greatest comebacks in bourbon history.

COLOR: Straw with hues of tan and sand

NOSE: This nose always reminds me of earth—a walk in the woods, where I smell oak, dirt, mushrooms, and the occasional fire. Of course, it also packs the usual caramel and vanilla notes.

PALATE: The notes on the nose find the palate nicely, but spice immediately expresses itself. Cinnamon, baking spices, and a warm, mouth-coating mouthfeel is felt all over the palate.

FINISH: This lovely medium finish offers subtle hints of cinnamon

COMPARE THOUGHTS
Did you think this was an earthy nose?

YOUR TASTING NOTES:

FOUR ROSES SMALL BATCH
Kentucky Straight Bourbon Whiskey

PROOF AND PRODUCT AGE: 90 proof. No age statement, but the product tends to be between 6 and 7 years old.

MASHBILL: Contains recipes OBSO, 35 percent; OBSK, 35 percent; OESO, 15 percent; and OESK, 15 percent (see recipe key on page 188)

BARRELS PER BOTTLING: 180. Regarding the amount of barrels used in Four Roses Small Batch, the master distiller Jim Rutledge explains: "All the barrels for Small Batch have been preassigned and tagged for Small Batch based on survey sampling of distillation lots and sensory evaluations starting at about four years age. The barrels are surveyed annually to confirm their targeted use for Small Batch. Prior to a bottling run, the individual barrels are sampled, and a Small Batch is blended in the quality control lab based on the prescribed recipe of the four bourbons used for Small Batch, and each barrel is sensory evaluated, as well as the blend, to ensure conformance to the targeted standard flavor profile—as close as possible. One of the reasons Small Batch barrels outnumber Yellow Label barrels is due to the age difference—small batch barrels are older, and there are less gallons per barrel."

COLOR: Rich caramel

NOSE: Perhaps no 2 products better represent a distillery's recipe goals than Four Roses Yellow Label and Small Batch. They couldn't smell more drastically different: Yellow Label's nose of earth and spice is contrasted by Small Batch's heavy nose of oak, cinnamon, floral, and fruit.

PALATE: The palate just warms up to gorgeous citrus, cinnamon, caramel, vanilla, and undertones of marshmallow, Chinese allspice, and fresh-baked apple pie. The chewy mouthfeel catches me a little off-guard toward the end, but Small Batch is a "flavor highway" sensation.

FINISH: Medium, with baking spices

COMPARE THOUGHTS
Was this spicy?

YOUR TASTING NOTES:

FOUR ROSES SINGLE BARREL
Warehouse AN / Barrel no. 43-6V

PROOF AND PRODUCT AGE: 100 proof. No age statement, but each barrel is between 7 and 8 years old.

MASHBILL: Recipe OBSV (see recipe key on page 188)

BARRELS PER BOTTLING: 1

COLOR: Dark caramel

NOSE: Toasted marshmallow, campfire smoke, canned pear, dried apricot, and cinnamon really come out of the glass strongly, but I'm left searching for a vanilla and caramel note. Will it be there in the palate?

PALATE: Oh, yes, there's the caramel and vanilla, followed by heavy spices and fruits. The creamy mouthfeel is enjoyable and leads to a lovely finish.

FINISH: This unexpectedly long finish rewards you with cinnamon, caramel, and vanilla.

COMPARE THOUGHTS
Were the caramel and vanilla missing in your aroma analysis?

YOUR TASTING NOTES:

CHAPTER NINE

SELECT LIMITED EDITIONS AND
SPECIAL RELEASES

Think back to your childhood. Was there a toy you really wanted but you could never get? Did a family member surprise you with the desired pony, Transformer, or special Barbie doll, only for you to be disappointed? Well, that is the story of limited-edition bourbons.

They can be overhyped, impossible to find, and not worth the money. Your liquor store will likely not have them in stock; if they do, you might be putting your name in a hat drawing or lottery, or you're paying 500 percent over the MSRP. Occasionally, you'll get your hands on these rare products, taste them, and feel chills trickle up your spine, making you think they're worth the money after all. In the end, these bourbons are for the hunter, one who is willing to brave the cold and risk coming up empty handed. I'm a bourbon hunter, as are thousands of other enthusiasts. Some bourbons in this chapter represent bourbon's very best; some are complete duds.

JELL-O SHOTS

3 boxes Jell-O with sugar
2¾ cups bourbon
3⅓ cups water

Bring the water to a boil, then remove it
from the heat and stir in the Jell-O until
dissolved. After 3 minutes, add bourbon
and stir. Pour the bourbon-laden liquid into
containers and freeze.

Due to the rarity and difficulty of finding the bourbons in this
chapter, I would not recommend making cocktails with them. But if you
do, you might as well make it fun. When the Louisville bar Meta made
Jell-O shots with the hard-to-find Pappy Van Winkle, I rather loved the
idea, so here's to wasting money on something fun! If you share photos
of these Jell-O shots containing the liquid gold, please be prepared for
an attack from the Whiskey Police.

BALCONES FIFTH ANNIVERSARY TEXAS STRAIGHT BOURBON WHISKEY

Texas Straight Bourbon Whiskey / Bottle no. 4 of 124 (bottled April 4, 2013)

DISTILLERY: Balcones Distillery, Waco, Texas

MASTER DISTILLER: Chip Tate, who is no longer the master distiller, made
this product. One of the first employees, Jared Himstedt, is now
the distiller.

PROOF AND PRODUCT AGE: 124 proof. 2 years old.

MASHBILL: 100 percent corn. Balcones uses commercial enzymes on all
100 percent corn mashes.

GRAIN ORIGINS: Midwestern blue corn

DISTILLATION: Double copper-pot stilled

BARREL ENTRY PROOF: 124.6

AGING: Balcones uses 225-liter American white oak barrels with a light toasting and light charring. The brand would not specify the barrel char when asked. Barrels are stacked for storage.

RELEASE TIMING AND HOW TO FIND: The Fifth Anniversary was one of the final products created by distiller and Balcones founder Chip Tate. He made subsequent bourbons, but this was his best. It was a one-time release and is extremely hard to find.

COLOR: Rich, offering hues of russet and caramel

NOSE: Nosing Balcones Fifth Year Anniversary is a little like working in a kitchen when someone is mixing cornbread. The smell of Jiffy cornbread batter fills the nose with profound hints of peach, apple, and jarred cherries.

PALATE: On the palate, the batter blossoms into the full-blown sweet taste of cornbread with a pat of creamy salted butter, followed by layers of caramel and vanilla with just a hint of a watermelon Jolly Rancher.

FINISH: For such a young, high-proof bourbon, Balcones finishes exceptionally smooth.

PAPPY VAN WINKLE 15-YEAR-OLD
Kentucky Straight Bourbon Whiskey

DISTILLERY: This is complicated. In an effort to save his family's legacy, Julian Van Winkle III and his father worked with the new owners of the Old Fitzgerald Distillery, who purchased the Stitzel-Weller Distillery from the Van Winkles in 1972 and renamed it Old Fitzgerald, to secure barrels of bourbon to continue the family line. He also purchased the Hoffman/Commonwealth Distillery in Lawrenceburg, Kentucky, accumulating more stocks and using the warehouse space as well as the bottling facilities, but he did not distill here. In 1992, his former family distillery closed, and in 2002, he entered a contract with the Buffalo Trace Distillery to begin distilling his family's wheated bourbon recipe. Van Winkle bourbons originally included barrels from several distilleries, but the core—the flavor-making bourbon anyway—was always from the family distillery with a touch of Lawrenceburg here and Buffalo Trace juice there. Now, that's gone or only a few drops remain. Van Winkle products 15 years and older may contain older stocks from distilleries past, but neither the family nor Buffalo Trace indicates how much Stitzel-Weller juice is left, so there's a bit of a mystery when you purchase a bottle.

MASTER BLENDER: Julian Van Winkle III. Van Winkle is not a distiller; he mingles or blends barrels of bourbon.

PROOF AND PRODUCT AGE: 107 proof. 15 years old.

MASHBILL: Wheated bourbon. This the same recipe used to create the Weller line at the Buffalo Trace Distillery (see page 165).

GRAIN ORIGINS: Post-2002, same as Buffalo Trace (see page 148)

DISTILLATION: Same as Buffalo Trace (see page 148)

BARREL ENTRY PROOF: 114

AGING: Pappy Van Winkle gets the pick of the barrel spots in Buffalo Trace warehouses.

RELEASE TIMING AND HOW TO FIND: Every fall and spring, liquor stores get their allocations of Pappy Van Winkle, which come in the form of Pappy 15, 20, and 23. Stores are lucky to get a single bottle and will hold auctions or lotteries for customers; some will sell them for as much as $6,000 per bottle. Sadly, bootleggers purchase every case they can and resell them through private Internet circles. The whole Pappy phenomenon is chaotic and incredibly unfair to you, the consumer. Your best bet to taste this bourbon is to fly to Louisville, where the local bourbon bars seemingly never run out of it. In fact, my Pappy 15 tasting notes come from the bottle at the Silver Dollar bar in Louisville. You can identify a pre-2007 Pappy Van Winkle bottle based on where it says it was bottled—if it's Lawrenceburg, Kentucky, it's from between 1989 and 2002; if it's Frankfort, Kentucky, it's 2002 to 2007. Post-2007 bottles indicate the date and time of bottling in the laser code on the back, below the label.

BARRELS PER BOTTLING: Unknown

COLOR: Deep, dark amber with gold hues

NOSE: So what's all the fuss about with this bourbon, right? Let's look at the nose. It's not jumping out of the glass like you'd expect if you believe in the hype. The nose is average, with oak, caramel, baked apples, brown sugar, honey, and melted, salted butter.

PALATE: This is where Pappy earns the hype. While the nose is average, the palate is a look into old-school whiskey with a drippingly good, mouth-coating mouthfeel, the whiskey slowly making its way around the jaw. The old notes are there, with caramel and vanilla custards leading the way and berry pies following, but it's how long they linger on your tongue that makes this one special. The caramel dances with your taste buds for a good 15 to 20 seconds, while other notes, such nutmeg, cinnamon, and dark cherry, surface along with hints of celery salt and oregano. This palate is like the Energizer Bunny—it just keeps on going.

FINISH: Extraordinary long, with a salted caramel note

ELIJAH CRAIG 21-YEAR-OLD
Kentucky Straight Bourbon Whiskey / Barrel no. 41

DISTILLERY: Heaven Hill Distillery. This product came from Heaven Hill's former Bardstown distillery, which burned to the ground in 1996.

MASTER DISTILLER: Parker Beam

PROOF AND PRODUCT AGE: 90 proof. 21 years old.

MASHBILL: For mashbill and other tech specs see page 140.

BARRELS PER BOTTLING: 1

RELEASE TIMING AND HOW TO FIND: This was a onetime release in 2013 but can occasionally be found in larger liquor stores that received a case. Heaven Hill has since released older Elijah Craigs than this one, but the 21-year-old remains the best.

COLOR: Deep, rich amber with golden hues

NOSE: The nose fully pronounces the style of great bourbons. It's complex, layered, and completely balanced, with cotton candy, vanilla cream, caramel, the freshly burnt crisp of crème brûlée, toffee, chocolate, and praline.

PALATE: Elijah Craig 21-Year-Old offers a baker's kitchen aroma, and the palate is like stepping inside the spice rack. The whiskey's velvety structure and creamy mouthfeel endure a juicy, somewhat fruity beginning before jumping right into a spice kick of cinnamon and nutmeg, the zest of orange peel, and toasted almond. Then, it gently brings the caramel, vanilla, and spice back to a warm, long finish. The whiskey just lingers.

FINISH: Long and lush, with vanilla

JIM BEAM SHERRY CASK

Bourbon Whiskey Finished in PX Sherry Casks / Distiller's MasterpieceDistillery: Jim Beam, Claremont, Kentucky

PROOF AND PRODUCT AGE: 100 proof. No age statement, but the bourbon was 12 years old before entering a sherry cask.

MASHBILL: Unknown; presumably Jim Beam's mashbill (see page 153).

GRAIN ORIGINS: Unknown

DISTILLATION: Double

BARREL ENTRY PROOF: Unknown

AGING: Beam takes 12-year-old bourbon and pours it into Pedro Ximenex (PX) sherry casks, where it sits for an undisclosed time.

RELEASE TIMING AND HOW TO FIND: The master's collections come out every fall, starting in 2013. This was the first.

BARRELS PER BOTTLING: Unknown

COLOR: Extremely deep amber

NOSE: Cream sherry, bananas, vanilla icing, dark-roast coffee, and dark fruits.

PALATE: The creamy mouthfeel certainly shows its sherry self, giving way to a characteristic sherry-like creaminess, almonds, and a slight brininess. This is followed by Fig Newton, smoke, an almost Scotch-like honey note, and hints of caramel and apple.

FINISH: Long and creamy

BUFFALO TRACE SINGLE OAK PROJECT

Kentucky Straight Bourbon Whiskey / Barrel no. 188

PROOF AND PRODUCT AGE: 90 proof.

MASHBILL, GRAIN ORIGINS, AND DISTILLATION: Same as Buffalo Trace (see page 148)

BARREL ENTRY PROOF: 105

AGING: This particular barrel was aged in the wooden ricks of Warehouse K, with a no. 4 barrel char after the staves were seasoned for 12 months.

BARRELS PER BOTTLING: 1

RELEASE TIMING AND HOW TO FIND: Since 2011, there have been 15 releases of the Single Oak Project, a study that analyzes the wood grains of 96 trees. Buffalo Trace made barrels from the top and bottom sections of the trees, studying the 192 unique sections. Staves were created from each section and air dried for 6 months or a year, then charred at no. 3 or 4 levels. The distillery has also studied the different barrel entry proof levels and different warehouse styles. A database has tracked the tasting profiles and differences, and Buffalo Trace has discovered nearly 1,400 tasting combinations among the 192 barrels. It's typically easy to find at least some of these products in high-volume bourbon stores in the United States, but finding all of them will be a challenge. This bottling, barrel no. 188, hit stores in February 2013.

COLOR: Amber

NOSE: Spicy with hints of chocolate and caramel. Fruits such as peach and apple express themselves toward the end.

PALATE: This is one of those bourbons for which the palate offers much more than the nose. It's rich with caramel, baking spice, vanilla custard, whipped cream, peach cobbler, Chinese allspice, and nutmeg, all with a crispy mouthfeel that tickles the tongue with citrus.

FINISH: Long, with a hint of orange

MICHTER'S TOASTED BOURBON

DISTILLERY, MASHBILL, GRAIN, AND DISTILLATION: Same as Michter's US 1 (see page 167)

AGING: For a onetime release, Michter's transferred its US 1 product to barrels seasoned 18 months and toasted to the company's specifications, but never charred like normal bourbon barrels.

RELEASE TIMING AND HOW TO FIND: This was the first barrel-finish release for the company. It should be available in most liquor stores that carry Michter's.

COLOR: Dark amber

NOSE: Oak, cinnamon, toffee, vanilla extract, almond extract, custard, and mint.

PALATE: There's a burnt grain in here, almost like blue corn chips or a sharp rye bread, but it's a welcome and unique note that you don't find often. There's also caramel, vanilla, marshmallow, praline, and a heavy dose of ginger toward the end of the chewy mouthfeel.

FINISH: Long, with hints of smoke

OKI RESERVE

Straight Bourbon Whiskey / Bottle no. 267 of 379 / Batch no. 4

DISTILLERY: Distilled at the MGP Ingredients Distillery in Lawrenceburg, Indiana, and bottled at the New Riff Distillery in Newport, Kentucky (a suburb of Cincinnati, Ohio).

MASTER DISTILLER: Greg Metze, MGP Ingredients. The New Riff blender is Jay Erisman.

PROOF AND PRODUCT AGE: 97.2 proof. 8 years old.

MASHBILL: 60 percent corn, 36 percent rye, and 4 percent malted barley

GRAIN ORIGINS: Likely Indiana and Kentucky for corn and the upper Midwest for rye.

DISTILLATION: Double distilled

BARREL ENTRY PROOF: 120

AGING: New Riff Distillery purchases barrels from MGP Ingredients 20 at a time and stores them in a Scottish-style stow. Shortly thereafter, these barrels are dumped to be bottled.

RELEASE TIMING AND HOW TO FIND: OKI is a celebration of the distillery's location. On the Kentucky-Ohio border, New Riff Distillery is sourcing whiskey from Indiana and bottling in a part of Kentucky that most locals consider Ohio. This tradition dates back to the 1800s, when distilleries sourced whiskey from Indiana. Thus, the name includes O for Ohio, K for Kentucky, and I for Indiana. OKI purchased a small assortment of 8-year-old MGP Ingredients barrels, which are among the oldest sourced from this location. The whiskey is uncut and unfiltered, and when this product is gone, this Indiana style at this age will be next to impossible to find. It's available at the distillery and in Ohio, Indiana, and Kentucky liquor stores.

BARRELS PER BOTTLING: 3 to 5

FILTERING METHOD: None

COLOR: Deep russet

NOSE: Beautiful nose of cherries, flowers, cinnamon, fresh-baked rye bread, and nutmeg.

PALATE: Spicy and warm, with lovely notes of black fruit jams, cornbread, caramel candies, vanilla-filled pastry, and a spicy note that follows the chewy mouthfeel to the finish.

FINISH: Long and filled with spice

WOODFORD RESERVE MASTER'S COLLECTION
Sonoma-Cutrer Finish

DISTILLERY: Woodford Reserve

MASTER DISTILLER: Chris Morris

PROOF AND PRODUCT AGE: 90.4 proof.

MASHBILL, GRAIN ORIGINS, AND DISTILLATION: Same as Woodford (see page 170).

AGING: Finished in Sonoma-Cutrer Pinot Noir barrels. Brown-Forman owns both brands.

RELEASE TIMING AND HOW TO FIND: The Master's Collection is an annual fall release of Woodford Reserve and changes one of the 5 sources of flavor every year. It's usually widely available.

BARRELS PER BOTTLING: Unknown

COLOR: Ultradark amber

NOSE: This nose will catch traditional bourbon drinkers off-guard. The Pinot Noir barrel certainly does its job here, offering up notes of cassis and loads of cherries. If not for the caramel and spice coming through, I wouldn't know this is a bourbon by its nose. A heavy oak bouquet finishes the nose.

PALATE: Unbalanced in the beginning, with one taste set pulling you toward the Pinot and the other trying to reel you back into the bourbon profile. For some, the palate might end there. But given the chance, the bourbon opens up with cherries—especially a turnover cherry pie—and caramel.

FINISH: Long and weird, finishing like a fruity Pinot

FOUR ROSES LIMITED EDITION SINGLE BARREL 2014
Kentucky Straight Bourbon Whiskey / Media sample

PROOF AND PRODUCT AGE: 120 proof, 11 years old

MASHBILL, GRAIN ORIGINS, DISTILLATION, AND AGING: Recipe OESF. See the Four Roses recipes and other tech specs on page 188.

RELEASE TIMING AND HOW TO FIND: Prior to 2015, Four Roses released 2 limited editions a year. Bourbon shortages forced them to discontinue the Limited Edition Single Barrel, making this 2014 vintage the last of its kind. Four Roses continues to release the Limited Edition Small Batch in the fall, and it is a perennial American Whiskey of the Year contender. Because of Four Roses' popularity, you should call your liquor store in advance to reserve a bottle.

COLOR: Dark amber

NOSE: Cinnamon, vanilla, caramel, toffee, melted butter, roasted almonds, and freshly baked pecan pie straight out of the oven. There are also some fun hints of earthiness, such as freshly cut grass, mushrooms, and tree bark.

PALATE: Warm, with a creamy mouthfeel, the bourbon swims down the jaw and gives a lesson in smoothness without a single burn. But boy, is it spicy! There's pepper, bell pepper, a slight bit of dried jalapeño, and a little cayenne in addition to the expected cinnamon and nutmeg spices. Of course, we cannot forget the vanillas and caramels—they're almost lost amidst the spice, but they're there.

FINISH: Long and spicy

BUFFALO TRACE ANTIQUE COLLECTION: EAGLE RARE 17-YEAR-OLD

For mashbill, aging, and other tech specs, see Buffalo Trace (page 148).

RELEASE TIMING AND HOW TO FIND: The Buffalo Trace Antique collection includes George T. Stagg, William Larue Weller, Eagle Rare 17-Year-Old, Sazerac Rye 18-Year-Old, and Thomas H. Handy Rye. They hit stores in the fall, but the limited supply forces liquor stores to be creative with how they sell them.

COLOR: Amber

NOSE: Orange zest, butter on toast, marshmallow, baked apples, warm cinnamon sticks, and hints of caramel and vanilla.

PALATE: Citrus, berries, and vanilla custard hit the taste buds immediately, settling the fully formed, mouth-coating mouthfeel that erupts into cinnamon sprinkled over a hot apple pie. Brown sugar, honey, and the vanilla custard follow this joy ride to the end.

FINISH: Long and lovely, with a vanilla custard finish

ORPHAN BARREL PROJECT: LOST PROPHET
Batch Tul-Tr-1 / Media sample

DISTILLERY: The Orphan Barrel Project is Diageo's series that bottles forgotten barrels. In the beginning, the company marketed these as "lost barrels," but in reality, they were never lost; taxes were paid on the barrels, after all. In reality, they were merely inventory not earmarked for a particular brand or sourced whiskey client. The Orphan Barrel bourbons include Old Blowhard, Barterhouse, Rhetoric, and Lost Prophet, and each has its own backstory. The

Lost Prophet was distilled at the former George T. Stagg facility in 1991 and aged at Stitzel-Weller.

MASTER DISTILLER: Gary Gayhart was the George T. Stagg distiller when this was made.

PROOF AND PRODUCT AGE: 90.1 proof. 22 years old.

MASHBILL: 75 to 78 percent corn, 7 to 10 percent barley, 15 percent rye

GRAIN ORIGINS: Unknown

DISTILLATION: Double

BARREL ENTRY PROOF: Unknown

AGING: Aged at the Stitzel-Weller facility.

RELEASE TIMING AND HOW TO FIND: The Orphan Barrel releases are limited, so their availability varies per market. However, some releases appear to have more store availability than others.

COLOR: Ultradark caramel

NOSE: A lovely nose of caramel, vanilla, bread pudding, cinnamon, nutmeg, allspice, campfire smoke, dark cherry jam, and honey. There's an unwanted nail-polish note in here, but the aforementioned notes mostly overshadow it.

PALATE: The palate dances with pumpkin spice, burnt caramel, vanilla latté, and an assortment of baking spices that range from nutmeg to allspice. The creamy mouthfeel coats the mouth with warmth.

FINISH: Long, with hints of cinnamon

OLD FORESTER BIRTHDAY BOURBON 2013

Media sample

For mashbill, aging, and other tech specs, see Old Forester (page 157).

PROOF AND PRODUCT AGE: 98 proof. No age statement.

RELEASE TIMING AND HOW TO FIND: Old Forester Birthday Bourbon is announced every year on September 2, the birthday of Brown-Forman founder George Garvin Brown. It's become a popular release but is still widely available where Old Forester is carried. That said, it's recommended to call your liquor store ahead of time.

COLOR: Deep amber

NOSE: Pear, oak, caramel, figs, sweet corn, vanilla, and toffee.

PALATE: Spicy, with a warm, creamy mouthfeel featuring hints of banana, strawberry, caramel, toffee, and sesame seeds.

FINISH: Short to medium, with hints of pumpkin

BRAND HISTORIES

1792 RIDGEMONT RESERVE

ESTABLISHED: 2002

OWNERS: Sazerac

NAME ORIGINS: 1792 is the year Kentucky joined the Union.

When Barton Brands Ltd. created the Ridgewood Reserve 1792 label, rival Brown-Forman filed a lawsuit that claimed it infringed upon the trademark of its Woodford Reserve brand. Barton changed its brand's name to 1792 Ridgemont Reserve, emphasizing 1792—the year Kentucky became a state—and changing Ridgewood to Ridgemont. Today, 1792 is one of Sazerac's flagship bourbons.

A. SMITH BOWMAN

ESTABLISHED: 1934

OWNERS: Sazerac

NAME ORIGINS: Named after its founder, A. Smith Bowman.

Like Kentucky, Virginia has a strong distilling history. Coming out of Prohibition, Kentuckian A. Smith Bowman built a distillery with his sons and started selling Virginia Gentleman Bourbon in 1937. In 2003, Sazerac purchased A. Smith Bowman.

From left to right, Wes, Lincoln, and Kyle Henderson. In this photo, the father-son-grandpa trio had just broken ground at its Louisville distillery, July 9, 2013. Founder Lincoln Henderson passed away a few months later.

ANGEL'S ENVY

ESTABLISHED: 2010

OWNERS: Bacardi

NAME ORIGINS: The 3 to 5 percent of bourbon lost per year due to evaporation, known as the "angel's share." Angel's Envy is the whiskey the angels didn't get.

Angel's Envy was the first mainstay bourbon product finished in port barrels, giving purist bourbon lovers headaches. How could it be called bourbon when used barrels are a staple of the brand's flavor profile? Simply put, the government allowed the company to do it as long as the label would say "straight bourbon finished in port barrels."

BAKER'S

ESTABLISHED: 1992

OWNERS: Beam Suntory

NAME ORIGINS: Named after Baker Beam, former distiller.

Baker Beam recalls working in the Jim Beam Distillery when somebody approached him about naming a bourbon after him. The year was 1985, and most bourbons were named after legends who'd passed away. "I was really surprised and honored," Baker told me. He became the Claremont distiller in 1973 when his father, Carl, retired from the same position.

BALCONES

ESTABLISHED: 2009

OWNERS: PE Investors LLC

NAME ORIGINS: The Balcones Fault Zone is responsible for the natural spring water from which the Waco, Texas, distillery draws its supply.

On July 17, 2013, Balcones announced new investors and a new distillery. The following year, the investors and founder Chip Tate were locked in a legal battle that resulted in Tate leaving the company. His partners bought him out in late 2014, and the Balcones legacy continues without its founder.

VERY OLD BARTON

ESTABLISHED: 1940s

OWNERS: Sazerac

NAME ORIGINS: Oscar Getz claims he picked "Barton" out of a hat.

Upon Prohibition's repeal, Oscar Getz and Lester Abelson started a whiskey company called Barton Brands, which would become one of the most powerful American-owned spirits companies of the twentieth century. Very Old Barton was marketed as high-end bourbon, with 1970s advertisements championing its age: "Very Old Barton spends eight long years aging (that's about four years longer than most bourbons) to become a smoother, mellower bourbon. So Very Old Barton gives you more bourbon flavor to give." Today, Very Old Barton is more of a value brand.

BASIL HAYDEN'S

ESTABLISHED: 1992

OWNERS: Beam Suntory

NAME ORIGINS: Named after Basil Hayden, famous Kentuckian.

When Anglo-American Catholics moved westward from Maryland, one of the leaders was a distiller named Basil Hayden. In 1785, Hayden was credited with leading twenty-five families down the Ohio River to Kentucky. His grandson, Raymond, created a brand called Old Grand Dad in his honor. Today, Beam Suntory owns Old Grand Dad and Basil Hayden's.

BELLE MEADE

ESTABLISHED: The modern company was created in 2006. Belle Meade hit shelves in 2011, but the family's history goes back to 1853.

OWNERS: Family owns the majority with a few angel investors.

NAME ORIGINS: Named after a former thoroughbred farm in the Nashville area.

During his day, the man behind the original Belle Meade Bourbon was as big as Jack Daniel, Jim Beam, E. H. Taylor, or any number of renowned bourbon producers. Based in Tennessee, Charles Nelson operated the Green Brier Distillery and produced about thirty labels,

The Buffalo Trace Distillery is located in Frankfort, Kentucky, and is a massive whiskey-making facility.

Tom Bulleit stands outside the Stitzel-Weller Distillery, which now serves as a Bulleit visitor center. Bulleit's parent company, Diageo, owns Stitzel-Weller and is also building a Bulleit distillery in Shelby, Kentucky.

two of them in conjunction with other companies. Established in 1853, the Charles Nelson Green Brier Distillery could have been what Jack Daniel's is today if not for Prohibition and a few business dealings not working in its favor. Thanks to a new Charles Nelson, Belle Meade is making a comeback.

BLANTON'S

ESTABLISHED: 1984

OWNERS: Age International

NAME ORIGINS: Named after Colonel Albert Blanton.

Colonel Albert Bacon Blanton was not alive to see his name on a bottle. He lived from 1881 to 1959, working as the superintendent and president at the George T. Stagg Distillery (now Buffalo Trace). Elmer T. Lee created Blanton's, the first so-called single barrel product available on liquor-store shelves.

BOOKER'S

ESTABLISHED: 1988

OWNERS: Beam Suntory

NAME ORIGINS: Named after Booker Noe.

The grandson of Jim Beam, Booker Noe started working in production at the distillery in 1951 and never left. He called the rack warehouse his second home and became a de facto bourbon ambassador, traveling the country talking nothing but bourbon. When he passed away in February 2004 at the age of seventy-four, the entire industry mourned a personality that could never possibly be replaced as well as a hound-like bourbon nose and palate that could find a honey barrel sitting nine barrels high.

BUFFALO TRACE

ESTABLISHED: 1999

OWNERS: Sazerac

NAME ORIGINS: Buffalo Trace is named after the buffalo finding passage across the Kentucky River en route to the Great Plains.

Buffalo Trace Distillery is one of the most important and historic distilleries in the United States, but the facility suffers from a century-old identity problem. While the George T. Stagg Distillery was renamed Buffalo Trace and the brand launched in 1999, the facility was also formerly the Ancient Age Distillery, and sections were the OFC Distillery. Locals continue to refer to Buffalo Trace as Ancient Age or Stagg. Nonetheless, Buffalo Trace Straight Bourbon ranks among the best introductory bourbons.

BULLEIT

ESTABLISHED: 1987

OWNERS: Diageo

NAME ORIGINS: Named after the Bulleit family.

When Tom Bulleit wrapped up his legal career and embarked on a new journey to start a bourbon company in the mid-1980s, he chose to create a bourbon brand that would change the face of bars around the world. The Bulleits built their demand the old-fashioned way: they knocked on doors and told their story. The hard work paid off, and its parent company is now building the $115 million Bulleit Distilling Company in Shelby County, Kentucky.

CYRUS NOBLE

ESTABLISHED: 1871

OWNERS: Haas Brothers, San Francisco

NAME ORIGINS: Nineteenth-century master distiller.

Of all the bourbons on the shelf today, Cyrus Noble enjoys one of the most colorful stories and is the only brand to have been featured on *Ripley's Believe It or Not!*. Noble, a three-hundred-pound distiller for the Bernheim Distillery, drank too much and fell into the mash bin, and Bernheim's partial owner, Ernest R. Lilienthal, wanted to name a whiskey after him. Lilienthal moved to San Francisco and started a company under his name, which later became Haas Brothers.

The creators of Devil's Cut came up with a catchy name and have offered even better television commercials, showing an illustration of the barrel being twisted and droplets of whiskey coming out.

DEVIL'S CUT

ESTABLISHED: 2011

OWNERS: Beam Suntory

NAME ORIGINS: Named after the whiskey trapped inside the wood—the angel gets the evaporation while the whiskey ages, and the devil gets his cut when the whiskey is dumped from the barrel.

Beam Suntory created an agitation method to extract whiskey trapped inside the freshly dumped barrel and called it Devil's Cut. It would probably be more appropriately named Barrel Sweat, the Kentucky term for taking a freshly dumped bourbon barrel, filling it with water, rolling it around the yard for a bit, allowing it to soak in the sunshine, and letting it sit bung-side down. But that would be likely to remind consumers of gym socks. Devil's Cut is much more appealing.

ELIJAH CRAIG

ESTABLISHED: 1986

OWNERS: Heaven Hill

NAME ORIGINS: The late 1700s Baptist preacher who earned the founder of bourbon moniker long before historians and journalists had a chance to scrutinize this claim.

When Heaven Hill launched the Elijah Craig brand in 1986, the popular bourbon company promoted the longstanding legend of its namesake inventing bourbon. As legends go, Craig supposedly discovered the barrel-charring technique in a barn fire. The story was so popular that television actor George J. McGee starred in the one-man play *The Life and Times of Elijah Craig* in 1982. These days, as social media dissects everything from high-fructose corn syrup to politics, people seemingly care about the whiskey truth-in-marketing. Thus, the Craig legend is just that, a legend—but it's a legend that helped build the bourbon industry, proving that whiskey loves a good story.

ELMER T. LEE

ESTABLISHED: 1986

OWNERS: Sazerac

NAME ORIGINS: Named after the former George T. Stagg distiller.

Old Fitzgerald master distiller Edwin Foote (left) and George T. Stagg master distiller Elmer T. Lee (center) greet country music star Neal McCoy at an outdoor bourbon event in the 1980s. Foote and Lee were among the great master distillers who brought bourbon back. *Photo courtesy Edwin Foote*

Elmer T. Lee is the distiller who almost wasn't. When he interviewed for the position, the venerable Colonel Blanton told him they weren't hiring, but the upright, hardworking World War II veteran stuck around and took the job anyway. Lee transformed the industry with Blanton's Single Barrel and his former distillery, Buffalo Trace, honors Lee's legacy with the brand donning his name and likeness.

EVAN WILLIAMS

ESTABLISHED: The original Evan Williams distiller began in 1783, but the actual brand was formed in 1957.

OWNERS: Heaven Hill Distillery

NAME ORIGINS: The Kentucky distiller of the 1780s.

In the 1780s, Evan Williams built a small distillery on Louisville's Fifth Street near the Ohio River, but he "claimed the right to sell his product without license" and was indicted by a grand jury for this offense.[3] Heaven Hill created the brand Evan Williams in 1957 and has since carved out a consistent bourbon for the ages.

FEW SPIRITS

ESTABLISHED: 2009

OWNERS: FEW Spirits

NAME ORIGINS: Talk about irony. FEW is named after Frances Elizabeth Willard, the founder of the Women's Christian Temperance Union.

Based in Evanston, Illinois, FEW Spirits is not too far from where the Women's Christian Temperance Union was founded. The WCTU was the leading voice in favor of Prohibition and the major reason why Evanston kept Prohibition in effect for four decades after the Volstead Act was repealed. The city remained dry until 1972, making it illegal to operate a distillery in the interim. When it opened in 2009, FEW Spirits became the first legal alcohol-production facility in Evansville since Prohibition.

FOUR ROSES

ESTABLISHED: 1888

OWNERS: Kirin Brewing in Japan

NAME ORIGINS: There are several stories that claim to explain why founder Paul Jones Jr. named this brand Four Roses. The brand sells the legend that Jones's hot date to a grand ball wore a four-rose corsage.

In the late 1950s, its parent company Seagram's took Four Roses Bourbon off the market and sent it into exile, casting it to foreign markets, where bourbon had zero marketing power. In 2001, Seagram's folded, and Japan-based Kirin Brewing purchased the brand. It kept the Seagram's methods and people and embarked on one of the greatest comebacks in American business history. Today, largely due to its five yeast strains, distillation methods, and single-story warehouses, Four Roses is arguably the sexiest distillery in Kentucky.

Four Roses offers private barrel selections to consumers, bars, and liquor stores, where you can taste samples like these straight from the barrel and choose your very own. Four Roses is based in Lawrenceburg, Kentucky.

GEORGE T. STAGG

ESTABLISHED: 2002

OWNERS: Sazerac

NAME ORIGINS: Like many names you see on the bottle, George T. Stagg was a major contributor to the growth of bourbon in the 1800s.

In the 1860s, George T. Stagg was a respected whiskey salesman and helped E. H. Taylor build his bourbon empire.

HENRY MCKENNA

ESTABLISHED: 1855

OWNERS: Heaven Hill

NAME ORIGINS: Named after an Irish immigrant and Kentucky distiller.

Henry McKenna moved from his native Ireland to Fairfield, Kentucky, starting a milling business and settiing up a pot still around 1855. McKenna served as his own cooper, milled and mashed his grains, and distilled, making him a master distiller and potentially a master cooper. According to the *Nelson Journal*, "what this horny-handed son of Old Ireland doesn't know about making Kentucky whiskey, no one knows."[4] Seagram's closed the Henry McKenna Distillery in the 1970s; Heaven Hill purchased the brand name but no longer uses the same recipe. The original yeast, mashbill, and flavor profile are gone. Lost with time.

HUDSON

ESTABLISHED: 2005

OWNERS: William Grant & Sons, London. Distilled at the original distillery, Tuthilltown Distillery in Gardiner, New York.

NAME ORIGINS: Named after the Hudson Valley area.

If you live in a US state without a significant distillery presence, you can thank Prohibition. The country is still recovering from the thirteen-year alcohol ban nearly a century after it ended, but states are coming around to opening distilleries again, thanks in part to Ralph Erenzo, cofounder of Tuthilltown Spirits. Hudson was Tuthilltown's flagship product; Hudson Baby Bourbon made such a splash that it garnered outside investor interest. William Grant & Sons, which owns a powerful Scotch whiskey portfolio, purchased the Hudson line in 2010.

When Hudson Baby Bourbon launched, the whiskey world didn't know what to do with itself, often resorting to a play on the former 1990s Pace Picante commercial line "Made in New York." But since its inception, Hudson has helped grow the bourbon category and the craft distillery movement.

JEFFERSON'S

ESTABLISHED: 1997

OWNERS: Castle Brands

NAME ORIGINS: Named after President Thomas Jefferson, who repealed the whiskey tax.

When Chet and Trey Zoeller created Jefferson's Reserve in 1997, the father-and-son duo received cease-and-desist letters from the lawyers of two major spirits companies, arguing the Jefferson's bottle was too similar to their brands. Although Chet was a successful attorney, the Zoellers didn't have the capital to fight the claim, and instead negotiated terms that made everybody happy—a new bottle. After this, the Jefferson's filled its new square bottles with bourbon procured from distillers throughout Kentucky.

As the thirteen millionth barrel of Jim Beam bourbon travels down the conveyor belt, dozens of reporters from around the world interview the great grandson of Jim Beam, Fred Noe. The Beams and Noes have carried bourbon through the good times and the bad.

JIM BEAM

ESTABLISHED: The Jacob Beam Distillery started in the 1790s without an official name, but the true Beam empire began in 1933.

OWNERS: Beam Suntory

NAME ORIGINS: Named after the real Jim Beam.

Bourbon could be called "Beam" and it would be a legitimate name for the whiskey. The Beams have been a part of more than sixty bourbon brands, including the Dowlings, Early Times, Heaven Hill, Limestone Branch, and Yellowstone. The greatest of them all was Col. Jim Beam, who started working in the distilling business at sixteen and later becoming president of Bardstown's F. G. Walker Distillery in 1913, which he operated along with the Clear Springs Distilling Company until Prohibition. Also prior to Prohibition, Jim Beam purchased the Old Murphy Barber Distillery to dig up the limestone rock as part of his family's stone business, registered as Sunbeam Quarries. The Claremont spot was located across from the newly formed Bernheim Forest, a fourteen-thousand-acre preserve established by fellow German immigrant and bourbon icon Isaac Wolfe Bernheim. Once Prohibition was repealed, Beam, at the age of seventy, used the Old Murphy Barber Distillery to create what is now known as the Jim Beam Distillery.

MAKER'S MARK

ESTABLISHED: 1953

OWNERS: Beam Suntory

NAME ORIGINS: Marjorie Samuels named Maker's Mark after pewtersmiths, who always left a so-called maker's mark on their work that identified them as the creator.

After he purchased the run-down Burks Springs Distillery in 1953, Bill Samuels Sr. and his wife, Marjorie, created Maker's Mark. He created the whiskey; she created the name, developed the slender bottle, and invented the now-iconic dripping red wax. The couple and their son, Bill Jr., are in the Bourbon Hall of Fame.

MB ROLAND

ESTABLISHED: 2009

OWNERS: Merry Beth and Paul Tomaszewski

NAME ORIGINS: Named after co-owner Merry Beth Roland.

During the rise of craft distilleries, or microdistilleries, Iraq War veteran Paul Tomaszewski asked a simple question: where were the microdistilleries in Kentucky? After his second tour of duty, Tomaszewski and his wife, Merry Beth Roland, opened the first distillery in Christian County, Kentucky, since Prohibition, converting a former Amish farm into the MB Roland Distillery in 2009.

MICHTER'S

ESTABLISHED: Like many things in whiskey, Michter's original founding date is complicated. The original Pennsylvania distillery site began in 1753, but the Michter's brand was not created until 1950. Since then, it's been on a rocky ride.

OWNERS: Chatham Imports

NAME ORIGINS: A combination of the names Michael and Peter, the founder's sons.

The original Michter's distillery sits barren in Schaefferstown, Pennsylvania, its parts picked and sold and used again. Listed on the prestigious National Register of Historic Places, the distillery was once an American whiskey crown jewel. Now, crows fly overhead and weeds grow on the edges of buildings. The site dates back to 1753, when John Shenk owned and operated a still; by 1780, the area was a hotbed for distilleries, with twenty stills in operation. George Washington allegedly purchased whiskey from the area to give to his troops. Today, Michter's operates in Kentucky and has released several stellar older whiskeys in the past decade.

Michter's began its legacy in Pennsylvania but today calls Kentucky its home.

OLD CHARTER

ESTABLISHED: 1867

OWNERS: Sazerac

NAME ORIGINS: Named after the charter oak, a now-extinct species.

Adam and Ben Chapeze inherited land along Long Lick Creek in Bardstown with intentions to farm. When the railroad built a station on the farm, the area became known as the Chapeze Station. Around this same time—1867—the brothers started the Chapeze Distillery, and they created the Old Charter brand in 1874. They sold their distillery to John Wright's and Marion Taylor's company in the early 1890s. Wright & Taylor grew Old Charter into one of the most formidable bourbon brands ever made, but Prohibition ended its prominence. In 1933, the Schenley's Bernheim Distillery purchased the Old Charter brand and the leftover stocks Wright & Taylor still had on its warehouse receipts, and Old Charter became one of the conglomerate's flagship bourbon brands along with I. W. Harper, Cascade, and Echo Spring. In 1999, the Sazerac Company, Buffalo Trace's parent, acquired Old Charter from United Distillers (which had acquired the Schenley Company more than ten years prior).

OLD CROW

ESTABLISHED: Mid-1800s

OWNERS: Beam Suntory

NAME ORIGINS: Named after the Scottish doctor James C. Crow, who pioneered many of the bourbon manufacturing methods in the 1800s.

Old Crow was named after the industry pioneer Dr. James C. Crow, who industrialized bourbon distilleries in the 1800s. One of the first brands to don a name, Old Crow was the undisputed best-selling bourbon before Prohibition and perhaps after. Mark Twain, Walt Whitman, and President Ulysses S. Grant were among the reported fans of Old Crow, and in 1966, a special bottling of Old Crow sold for $5,000 (equivalent to $35,900 in 2014) to benefit the Society of the Preservation of the Crow. When Fortune Brands purchased National Distillers, who owned Old Crow, in 1987, the brand became less representative of its former glory.

OLD FITZGERALD

ESTABLISHED: 1870 under S. C. Herbst through Prohibition

OWNERS: Heaven Hill

NAME ORIGINS: Named after either treasury agent John. E. Fitzgerald or a former employee.

When S. C. Herbst founded his company in 1870, he created two businesses. One was a thriving wine and spirits import company that brought to the US market A. De Luze & Fils, which made cognac, Bordeaux wines, claret, and sauternes. The other side of the business was bourbon. Herbst initially contracted the J. Swigert Taylor Distillery to make "Jn. E. Fitzgerald," but in the early 1890s, the S. C. Herbst company purchased the Old Judge Distillery and renamed it the Old Fitzgerald Distillery. The origins of this name remain a mystery, with some saying the namesake was a Herbst employee with keen distilling skills. In the book *Always Fine Bourbon* by Sally Van Winkle Campbell—whose grandfather, Pappy, and his company, Stitzel-Weller, purchased Old Fitzerald during Prohibition—the author argues the real Fitzgerald was a crooked government agent. Nonetheless, Old Fitzgerald is likely to be remembered as one of Pappy Van Winkle's brands that left his family's control when they sold the distillery in 1972 to Norton-Simon, who sold it to Distillers Limited in 1984. In 1992, Heaven Hill acquired Old Fitzgerald and it's now made at the Bernheim Distillery, a few miles from the former Stitzel-Weller plant.

OLD FORESTER

ESTABLISHED: 1870

OWNERS: Brown-Forman

NAME ORIGINS: Named after Dr. William Forrester, a popular Louisville physician who frequently prescribed this particular whiskey. After Forrester retired, the second "r" was dropped from the brand's spelling.

In 1870, brothers George Garvin Brown and J. T. S. Brown Jr. formed a whiskey firm with Old Forester as their brand and sold exclusively by the bottle. They were chasing the pharmaceutical market; although whiskey was a popular medicine, doctors were purchasing barrels, which were diluted for greater wholesaler profits. The Browns realized whiskey purchasers wanted assurance that what they were buying was actually 100 percent whiskey, not 60 percent whiskey, 20 percent

Uncle Joe's tobacco spit, and 20 percent Great-Grandma's prune juice. So, Old Forester became the first exclusively bottled bourbon, giving purchasers trust that the whiskey was really whiskey. It helped that the bottle was more convenient to prescribe than drawing doses from a barrel. In 1902, George Garvin Brown created Brown-Forman, which still owns Old Forester.

PAPPY VAN WINKLE

ESTABLISHED: In the 1970s, the Van Winkles resurrected the pre-Prohibition label Old Rip Van Winkle and later added Pappy Van Winkle to the lineup. The iconic photo of Pappy smoking a cigar did not appear on a brand label until 1995.

OWNERS: Partnership between the Van Winkle family and Sazerac.

NAME ORIGINS: Named after the former whiskey salesman and founder of the Stitzel-Weller Distillery.

Julian P. "Pappy" Van Winkle Sr. started as a W. L. Weller and Sons salesman, selling the brand names Old W. L. Weller, Mammoth Cave, Cabin Still, Harlem Club, Hollis Rye, Silas B. Johnson, and Stone Root Gin. In 1908, Van Winkle and fellow salesman Alex T. Farnsley purchased the Weller wholesale business. When Prohibition hit, Van Winkle and Farnsley locked up their facilities and walked away. They attempted to start another business, losing significant money in a farm-equipment company. Van Winkle, Farnsley, and A. Ph. Stitzel also formed the American Medicinal Spirits Company to offer their existing whiskey stocks to physicians. Meanwhile, doctors were prescribing whiskey at an alarming rate. When Prohibition ended, the three men formed the Stitzel-Weller Distillery, opening the facility on Kentucky Derby Day 1935. Van Winkle became bourbon's heart, changing the game in so many ways. He helped pioneer the private label business and wrote advertorials long before they taught the tactic in college. Pappy died in 1965.

REDEMPTION

ESTABLISHED: 2010

OWNERS: Bardstown Barrel Selections

NAME ORIGINS: Named after the founders' personal redemption.

Redemption is the brainchild of two spirits-industry veterans who have made a lot of money for other spirits companies through consulting and marketing efforts. Business partners Michael Kanbar and Dave Schmier provided bottling solutions for smaller distilleries, and Schmier is the founder of the Independent Spirits Expo. This brand represents their career Redemption.

TOWN BRANCH

ESTABLISHED: 2011

OWNERS: Alltech

NAME ORIGINS: Named after an underground creek.

Despite being in the heart of bourbon country, the city of Lexington, Kentucky, has really lost its distilling prowess. The Henry Clay Distillery (named after the Kentucky statesman), James E. Pepper Distillery, Ashland Distillery, Tarr Distillery, and Lexington Distillery were among the companies that spread bourbon throughout horse country in the 1800s. Fires and Prohibition decimated Lexington's distillery community, but the Town Branch Distillery looks to restore its rich heritage.

Pappy Van Winkle once convinced Conrad Hilton to buy his whiskey as a private label for the Hilton Hotel Chain. Now, his name and likeness are used to sell the world's most coveted bourbon, so rare the Hiltons of the world can't even find it. *Photo courtesy of Buffalo Trace*

Wild Turkey has not changed its recipe once, but it has tinkered with its proofs. The 101- and 81-proof bourbons are symbolic of past changes.

WELLER

ESTABLISHED: 1849

OWNERS: Sazerac

NAME ORIGINS: Named after William Larue Weller.

William Larue Weller began his whiskey journey as a rectifier. In 1852, his firm advertised in the *Louisville Daily Journal* that it specialized in "rectified whiskey and foreign and domestic liquors."[9] The Weller family also dabbled in the cologned-spirits business and in making gin, and they used their still to produce high wines for blending. But a significant fire in the 1870s destroyed their Main Street facility. In the modern era, after the Van Winkle ownership of Weller, Sazerac acquired the Weller brand from United Distillers in 1999. Today, Weller is considered the poor man's Pappy Van Winkle, since it uses the same mashbill recipe but has different ages.

WILD TURKEY

ESTABLISHED: 1940s

OWNERS: Campari

NAME ORIGINS: Named after a wild turkey hunt.

In the early 1940s, the Austin Nichols president Thomas McCarthy would draw whiskey from premium barrels in the Anderson County Distillery or Old Ripy warehouses and take them with him on his wild turkey hunts. His friends would ask, "Hey, when are you going to get more of that wild turkey bourbon?" The name sort of stuck, and Wild Turkey was born. Today, the brand is owned by Campari, which invested more than $100 million to build a new distillery and visitor center.

WILLETT BRANDS

ESTABLISHED: First established in 1935. Closed in early 1980s, reorganized in 1984 under Even Kulsveen as Kentucky Bourbon Distillers.

OWNERS: Family owned.

NAME ORIGINS: Willett is the family surname. Rowan's Creek is named after a creek at the bottom of the hill of the distillery; the creek in turn is named after John Rowan, a Kentucky statesman who lived from 1773 to 1843. Noah's Mill is a name made up by the modern owners. Johnny Drum is named after a young Civil War soldier. Contrary to popular belief, Old Bardstown takes its moniker not from the town of Bardstown but from the bay gelding of the same name that retired with $628,752 in race winnings.

The Willett family of whiskeys includes Johnny Drum, Kentucky Vintage, Old Bardstown, Noah's Mill, Pure Kentucky, Rowan's Creek, and, of course, Willett. These products don't sit on shelves long, for they evoke the same sense of emotion and consumer loyalty as the greatest bourbons ever made. What's interesting about this is the Willett Distillery, also known as Kentucky Bourbon Distillers, only started distilling its own products in 2012.

WOODFORD RESERVE

ESTABLISHED: 1996

OWNERS: Brown-Forman

NAME ORIGINS: Named after the county in which it resides.

In the 1990s, Brown-Forman repurchased the Oscar Pepper distillery site it once owned and commenced a $10 million rebuilding project. Since then, Woodford Reserve has grown quickly, amassing a following of consumers who are not simply bourbon drinkers but "Woodford drinkers."

Willett bourbons are among the most treasured and sought after. Fans can rest assured that this will likely continue as long as the distillery is led by Drew Kulsveen (pictured) and his family. Kulsveen is considered to be among the brightest young people in the spirits business.

NOTES

SECTION ONE

1. Veach, 22
2. Jefferson, 109
3. Corlis Papers, Filson Historical Society
4. *The Kentucky Encyclopedia*, 228
5. Lehmann, 262
6. Veach, 24
7. US Congress, 47–48
8. "Annual Report of the Commissioner of Indian Affairs," 94
9. Wagner, 171
10. "Slave Trade," 26
11. Pearce, 11
12. Young, 166
13. Portions of this sidebar appeared in my *Whisky Advocate* story about bourbon taxes.
14. "New Whiskey Ruled Out for Rest of Year," 9
15. US Congress, 21

SECTION TWO

1. Edstrom, Ed. "Nice Work if You Can Get It." *St. Louis Globe-Democrat*, May 31, 1943. Section C, page 1.
2. This quote originally appeared in my *Whisky Advocate* coverage regarding barrel wood forestry.

SECTION THREE

1. Hennesey, 81
2. *Bonforts Wine and Spirit Circular*, no. 212, October 10, 1883.
3. Filson Club, 79
4. *Life*, R4
5. Pacult, F. Paul, *American Still Life: The Jim Beam Story and the Making of the World's #1 Bourbon* (Wiley, 2003). Page 164.
6. Lowery, Steve, "Noe Bourbon for Him." *Kentucky Standard*, April 11, 1988. Page 3.
7. Carson, Gerald, *The Social History of Bourbon* (University Press of Kentucky, 2010).
8. Veach, 53
9. Van Winkle Campbell, Sally, *But Always Fine Bourbon: Pappy Van Winkle and the Story of Old Fitzgerald* (Limestone Lane Press, 1999). Page 22.
10. Portions of this Woodford Reserve biography were originally published in my tasting-panel coverage of the brand.

BIBLIOGRAPHY

"Annual Report of the Commissioner of Indian Affairs." Washington, DC: Government Printing Office, 1862.

Bolles, Albert Sidney. *Industrial History of the United States.* Norwich, CT: The Henry Bill Publishing Company, 1889.

Brown, George Garvin. *The Holy Bible Repudiates Prohibition.* Louisville: George Garvin Brown, 1910.

Carson, Gerald. *The Social History of Bourbon.* New York: Dodd, Mead, 1963.

Cecil, Sam K. Bourbon: *The Evolution of Kentucky Whiskey.* Nashville: Turner Publishing, 2010.

Clark, Thomas D. "Corn Patch and Cabin Rights." In *The Kentucky Encyclopedia.* Lexington, KY: University Press of Kentucky, 1992.

"Commissioner of Revenue for the Fifth District of Tennessee." Edited by *Bonfort's Wine and Spirit Circular*, 212, 1883.

Cowdery, Charles K. *Bourbon, Straight: The Uncut and Unfiltered Story of American Whiskey.* Chicago: Made and Bottled in Kentucky, 2004.

The Filson Club, Reuben Thomas Durrett, and Henry Thompson Stanton. *The Centenary of Kentucky.* Louisville: John P. Morton & Company, 1892.

Frey, Charles N. "Background and Basic Principles, History of the Development of Active Dry Yeast." In *Yeast: Its Characteristics, Growth, and Function in Baked Products.* Chicago: Quartermaster Food and Container Institute for the Armed Forces, 1955.

"New Whiskey Ruled Out for Rest of Year." Joplin Globe, September 16, 1943.

"Here's a Pipeful of Common Sense About Whiskey." Advertisement. *Life*, June 7, 1937.

Hilsebusch, Henry William. *Knowledge of a Rectifier*. Providence, RI: The Gem Publishing, 1904.

Jefferson, Thomas. "To Colonel Charles Yancey," January 6, 1816. In *Selected Letters of Thomas Jefferson*.

Krass, Peter. *Blood and Whiskey: The Life and Times of Jack Daniel*. New York: Wiley, 2004.

Lehmann, Karl Bernhard. *Methods of Practical Hygiene*, vol. 2. London: Kegan Paul, Trench, Trubner & Co.

M'Harry, Samuel. *The Practical Distiller, or, an Introduction to Making Whiskey, Gin, Brandy*. Harrisburgh, PA: John Wyeth, 1809.

Marston, A. J., MD. "Spiritus Frumenti." *Eastern Medical Journal*. 4:12, 1885.

"Old Crow Begins with Men Who Love to Work with Their Hands." Advertisement. *Life*, October 27, 1970.

Owens, Bill. *The Art to Distilling Whiskey and Other Spirits*. New York: Crestline Books, 2012.

Pearce, John Ed. *Divide and Dissent: Kentucky Politics, 1930–1963*. Lexington, KY: University Press of Kentucky, 1987.

"Slave Trade. Papers Relating to Slaves in the Colonies; Slaves Manumitted; Slaves Imported, Exported; Manumissions . . ." House of Commons, 1826–1827.

US Congress. "Senate Documents, Otherwise Publ. As Public Documents." Edited by the Sixteenth Congress. Washington, DC: Gales & Seaton, 1819.

Vazsonyi, Andrew. *Which Door Has the Cadillac: Adventures of a Real-Life Mathematician*. Lincoln, Nebraska: iUniverse, 2002.

Veach, Michael R. *Kentucky Bourbon Whiskey: An American Heritage*. Lexington, KY: University Press of Kentucky, 2013.

Wagne, Leopold. *More About Names*. London: T. Fisher Unwin, 1893.

Young, James Harvey. *Pure Food: Securing the Federal Food and Drugs Act of 1906*. Princeton, NJ: Princeton University Press, 1989.

Zoeller, Chester. *Bourbon in Kentucky: A History of Distilleries in Kentucky*. Louisville: Butler Books, 2009.

INDEX

ABOUT THE AUTHOR

Wall Street Journal best-selling author Fred Minnick wrote the award-winning *Whiskey Women: The Untold Story of How Women Saved Bourbon, Scotch and Irish Whiskey*. Minnick writes about whiskey for *Covey Rise*, *Parade*, *Scientific American*, *Whisky Advocate*, and *Whisky* magazine. He is the "bourbon authority" for the Kentucky Derby Museum and regularly appears in the mainstream media, including *CBS This Morning*, *Esquire*, *Forbes*, and NPR.

ACKNOWLEDGMENTS

I want to first thank all the whiskey geeks out there who attend my Kentucky Derby Museum events, read my work, and converse with me on Twitter and Facebook. Without your interest and constant questioning of brands, I couldn't have written this book.

To my literary agent, Linda Konner, you're the best in the business, and one day, I'll get you to like bourbon.

A big thank-you to my Quarto editor, Dr. Elizabeth Demers, who saw something in my work long before anybody knew my name. This marks the second book she's acquired from me. And to Quarto's Madeleine Vasaly, thank you for your incredible edits.

Thank you to Paul Hletko, Mike Veach, Denny Potter, Drew Kulsveen, attorney Edwin Vargas, and Dave Schmier for fact-checking sections of my manuscript and to whiskey geek Chris Huss for offering up his bottles for a photo shoot.

A huge—and I mean huge—thanks goes to Heaven Hill for allowing me unprecedented access to its corn growers and distillery operations. Buffalo Trace, Brown-Forman, Heaven Hill, MB Roland, Hudson Bourbon, Balcones, and Finger Lakes Distilling provided samples for the tasting section, while the legendary Silver Dollar bourbon bar kindly let me sample products directly from its shelf.

Lastly, but certainly not least, to my lovely wife, Jaclyn, thank you for the ongoing support. You're truly the best.